Understanding Statistics
A Guide for
I/O Psychologists
and Human Resource Professionals

Michael G. Aamodt
Radford University and DCI Consulting

Michael A. Surrette
Springfield College

David Cohen
DCI Consulting

THOMSON
™
WADSWORTH

Australia • Brazil • Canada • Mexico • Singapore • Spain • United Kingdom • United States

Printed in the United States of America

2 3 4 5 6 7 10 09 08 07

Printer: ePAC

ISBN 978-0-495-18663-2

ISBN 0-495-18663-5

Thomson Higher Education
10 Davis Drive
Belmont, CA 94002-3098
USA

For more information about our products, contact us at:
Thomson Learning Academic Resource Center
1-800-423-0563

For permission to use material from this text or product, submit a request online at
http://www.thomsonrights.com.
Any additional questions about permissions can be submitted by e-mail to
thomsonrights@thomson.com.

Contents

Introduction and Acknowledgments

THE PURPOSE OF THIS BOOK is to provide students and human resource professionals with a brief guide to understanding the statistics they encounter in journal articles, technical reports, and conference presentations. If we accomplish our goals, you won't panic when someone uses such terms as t test or analysis of variance, you won't have a puzzled look during conference presentations, and you will actually comprehend most of the statistics you encounter. What you won't be able to do after reading this book is compute these statistics by hand. If that is your goal, there are plenty of good statistics books available that can teach you how to do this.

Chapter 1 provides an overview of why statistical analysis is conducted and covers a few important points such as significance levels. Chapter 2 explains the basic statistics used to describe data such as measures of central tendency (mean, median, mode), measures of dispersion (variance, standard deviation), and standard scores. Chapter 3 covers statistics used to determine group differences such as t tests, analysis of variance, and chi-square. Chapter 4 discusses correlation and how to interpret correlation coefficients. Chapter 5 covers regression analysis. Chapter 6 explains meta-analysis, a statistical method for reviewing the literature. Chapter 7 concludes the discussion of statistics by covering factor analysis.

Though there are plenty of other statistics out there, we wanted to cover the statistics most frequently encountered by human resource professionals. To help readers apply what they have learned, we have included references in each chapter to journal articles that have used the statistic covered by the chapter. When possible, we tried to use journal articles from *Public Personnel Management*, the journal published by the International Personnel Management Association for Human Resources or *Applied H.R.M. Research*, the on-line journal (www.radford.edu/~applyhrm) published by Radford University and the International Public Management Association Assessment Council (IPMAAC). When possible, we also tried to use some humor, at least as much as is possible when talking about statistics.

To break the monotony of reading about statistics, the names of television or movie characters are listed as employees in the various tables. Try to identify the television shows or movies that they represent.

We would like to thank Johnny Fuller and Keli Wilson of DCI Consulting, Pete Aponte of IBM, Dan Biddle of Biddle Consulting, and Bobbie Raynes of New River Community College for their help in reviewing this book and providing valuable feedback.

If you have any questions, would like to comment on the book, or find an error, please feel free to contact Mike Aamodt (maamodt@radford.edu).

1. The Concept of Statistical Analysis

AS WE START THE 21st century, it is obvious that the field of human resources has become more complex. It seems that we can't read a journal article, listen to a conference presentation, or talk to a consultant without encountering some form of statistical analysis. Though actually computing many statistics can be a complex process, understanding most journal articles or conference presentations should not be. At times it may appear that there are five million types of statistics, but statistical analyses are done for only one of four reasons: to describe data, determine if two or more groups differ on some variable (e.g., test scores, job satisfaction), determine if two or more variables are related, or to reduce data. This chapter will briefly explain these reasons as well as explain some of the basics associated with statistical analysis. Each of the following chapters will explain in greater detail the statistics mentioned in this chapter.

Reasons for Analyzing Data

TO DESCRIBE DATA

The most simple type of statistical analysis—descriptive statistics—is conducted to describe a series of data. For example, if an employee survey was conducted, one might want to report the number of employees who responded to each question (sample size), how the typical employee responded to each question (mean, median, mode), and the extent to which the employees answered the questions in similar ways (variance, standard deviation, range). These types of descriptive statistics will be discussed in detail in Chapter 2.

TO DETERMINE IF TWO OR MORE GROUPS DIFFER ON SOME VARIABLE

Once descriptive statistics are obtained, a commonly asked question is whether two groups differ. For example, did women perform better in training than men? Were older employees as likely to accept a new benefit plan as their younger counterparts? To answer such questions, we would use:

- A *t-test* if there were only two groups (e.g., male, female) and our descriptive statistic was a mean.
- An *analysis of variance* if our descriptive statistic was a mean and there were more than two groups (e.g., south, north, east, west) or more than one independent variable (e.g., race and gender).
- A *chi-square* if our descriptive statistic was a frequency count.

These statistics will be discussed in detail in Chapter 3.

TO DETERMINE IF TWO OR MORE VARIABLES ARE RELATED

A question often asked in research is the extent to which two or more variables are related, rather than different. For example, we might ask if a test score is related to job performance, if job satisfaction is related to employee absenteeism, or if the amount of money spent on recruitment is related to the number of qualified applicants. To determine if the variables are related, we might use a *correlation*. If we wanted to be a bit more precise or are interested in how several different variables predict performance, we might use *regression* or *causal modeling*. Correlation will be discussed in greater detail in Chapter 4 and regression in Chapter 5.

TO REDUCE DATA

At times, we have a lot of data that we think can be simplified. For example, we might have a 100-item questionnaire. Rather than separately analyze all 100 questions, we might check to see if the 100 questions represent five major themes/categories/factors. To reduce data, we might use a *factor analysis* or a *cluster analysis*. Factor analysis will be discussed in detail in Chapter 6.

Significance Levels

Significance levels are one of the nice things about statistical analysis. If you are reading an article about the effectiveness of a new training technique and don't care a thing about statistics, you can move through the alphabet soup describing the type of analysis used (e.g., ANOVA, MANOVA, ANACOVA) and go right to the significance level which will be written something like, "$p < .03$." What this is telling you is that the difference in performance between two or more groups (e.g., trained versus untrained or men versus women) is significantly different at some level of chance.

What is the need for significance levels? Suppose that you walk into a training room and ask the people on the right side of the room how old they are and then do the same to people sitting on the left side of the room. You find that the average age of the people sitting on the right side of the room is 37.6, whereas the average age of people on the left side of the room is 39.3 years. Does this difference make you want to submit a paper on the subject? Could it be that older people sit closer to the door so they don't have to walk as far? It could be, but probably not. Anytime we collect data from two or more groups, the numbers will never be identical. The question then becomes, if the numbers are never identical, how much of a difference does it take before we can say that something is actually happening? This is where significance levels come in. Based on a variety of factors such as sample size and variance, the end result of any statistical analysis is a significance level that indicates the probability that our results occurred by chance alone. If our analysis indicates that the groups differ at $p < .03$, then we would conclude that there are 3 chances in 100 that the differences we obtained were the result of fate, karma, or chance. In the social sciences, we have a very dumb rule that if the probability is less than 5 in 100 that our results could be due to chance ($p < .05$), we say that our results are statistically significant.

CHOOSING A SIGNIFICANCE LEVEL

Although .05 is the significance level traditionally used in the social sciences, in some circumstances researchers may choose to use a more liberal or a more conservative level. This choice is a function of the cost associated with being wrong. When interpreting the results of a statistical analysis, there are two ways in which an interpretation can be wrong: a Type I error and a Type II error. To explain these errors, let's imagine a study in which a personnel analyst is trying to predict job performance by using an employment test.

With a *Type I* error, the researcher concludes that there is a relationship between the test and job performance when in fact there is no such relationship. With a *Type II* error, the researcher concludes that there is no relationship between the two variables when in fact there is one. By using a more conservative significance level such as .01 or .001, a researcher is trying to reduce the chance of a Type I error. Likewise, by using a more liberal significance level such as .10 or .15, a researcher is trying to reduce the chance of a Type II error.

The decision to use a particular significance level is determined by the cost of being wrong. If the employment test is expensive to administer and might result in the hiring of fewer women and minorities, our personnel analyst might want to use a conservative significance level (e.g., .01) to reduce the chance of a Type I error. That is, if we are going to spend a great deal of money to use a test that might also decrease the diversity of our workforce, we want to be very sure that the test actually predicts performance. However, suppose the test costs 20 cents per applicant and does not result in adverse impact, we might be more willing to make a Type II error—using a test that doesn't actually predict performance. If this were the case, we might be willing to accept a significance level of .10.

In addition to considering the financial and social costs of being wrong, significance levels can be selected on the basis of previous research. That is, if 50 previous studies found a significant relationship between an employment test and job performance, we might be more willing to consider a probability level of .07 to "be significant" than we would if there were no previous studies.

Statistical significance levels only tell us if we are allowed to "pay attention" to our results. They do not tell us if our results are important or useful. If our results are statistically significant, we get to interpret them and make decisions about "practical significance". If they are not statistically significant, we start again.

STATISTICAL SIGNIFICANCE IN JOURNAL ARTICLES

Statistical significance levels are usually presented in journal articles or conference papers in one of two ways. The first way is to list the significance level in the text. For example, an article might read:

> *The job satisfaction level of female employees (M=4.21) was significantly higher than that of male employees (M=3.50), t(60) = 2.39, p < .02.*

The $M = 4.21$ and $M = 3.50$ are mean scores on a job satisfaction scale, the 60 is the degrees of freedom (you will learn about this in chapter 3), the 2.39 is the value of the t-test (you will learn about this in chapter 3), and the $p < .02$ tells us that there are only 2 chances in 100 that we would expect similar results purely by chance. In other words, the difference

5

in satisfaction between men and women is statistically significant.

The second way to depict a significance level is to use asterisks in a table. Take for example the numbers shown in Table 1.1. The correlation of .12 between cognitive ability and commendations does not have any asterisks, indicating that it is not statistically significant. The correlation between education and commendations has one asterisk indicating that the correlation is significant at the .05 level. The correlation between education and performance in the police academy has two asterisks indicating that it is significant at the .01 level, and the three asterisks above the .43 indicate that the correlation between cognitive ability and academy performance is significant at the .001 level of confidence. The greater the number of asterisks, the greater the confidence we have that the number did not occur by chance.

Practical Significance

If our results are statistically significant, we then ask about the "practical significance" of our findings. This is usually done by looking at *effect sizes*, which can include *d scores*, *correlations (r)*, *omega-squares*, and a host of other awful sounding terms. Effect sizes are important to understand because we can obtain statistical significance with large sample sizes but have results with no practical significance.

Table 1.1
Example of statistical significance

	Academy Score	Commendations
Cognitive ability	.43***	.12
Education	.28**	.24*

* $p < .05$, ** $p < .01$, *** $p < .001$

For example, suppose that we conduct a study with a million people and find that women score an average of 86 on a math test and men score an average of 87. With such a big sample size, we would probably find the difference between the two scores to be *statistically* significant. However, what would we conclude about the *practical* significance of a one-point difference between men and women on a 100-point exam? Are men "superior" to women in math? Will we have adverse impact if we use a math test for selection? Should we discourage our daughters from a career in science? Probably not. The statistical significance allows us to confidently say that there is little difference between men and women on this variable. If we compute an effect size, we can say this in a more precise way.

Types of Measurement

Statistical data come in four measurement types: nominal, ordinal, interval, and ratio, which can easily be remembered with the acronym NOIR (if for some reason you actually want to remember these four types). Understanding the four measurement types is important because the four measurement types are often mentioned in journal articles and certain types of statistical analyses can only be performed on certain types of data.

Nominal data consist of categories or dimensions and have no numerical meaning by themselves. Examples of nominal data include race, hair color, and marital status. When nominal data are included in a data set, it is common to assign a numerical code to each of the categories. An example of assigning numbers to nominal data for hair color might be 1=blond, 2=brunette, 3=brown, 4=black, 5=red. As you can see from this example, the numbers assigned to categories have no real meaning. That is, a hair color of 5 is not a "better" hair color than a hair color of 1. Likewise, saying that the mean hair color of our sample is 3.3 would be meaningless. Instead, the numerical code is just shorthand for the category description. In human resources we often see such coding for race (i.e., 1=White, 2=African American, 3=Hispanic, 5=Asian) and sex (1=male, 2 = female).

Ordinal data are rank orders. Examples of ordinal data include baseball standings ("Who's in first place?"), seniority lists ("She is third from the top), and budget requests ("Put in rank order your list of needed equipment and we will see what we can purchase."). Ordinal data tell us the relative difference between people or categories but do not tell us anything about the absolute difference between the people or the categories. For example, if applicants are placed on a hiring list on the basis of their test scores, we know that the person ranked first has a higher score than the person ranked second; but we don't know if the difference between the two is one point or 50 points. Likewise, as shown in Table 1.2, the score difference between the applicants in first and second place is not necessarily the same score difference between the applicants in second and third place.

Interval data have equal intervals but not necessarily equal ratios. Examples of interval data include performance ratings, the temperature outside, and a score on a personality test. Let's use temperature to demonstrate. A thermometer has equal intervals in that the distance between 89 and 90 degrees and the distance between 54 and 55 degrees is the same (one degree). However, a temperature of 80 degrees is not "twice as hot" as a temperature of 40 degrees. Thus, although the intervals between points on the sale are equal, the ratio is not.

Ratio data have equal ratios and a true zero point. Examples of ratio data include salary, height, and the number of job applicants. All three have a true zero point in that someone can have no salary, there can be no job applicants, and if something doesn't exist, it can have no height. The ratios are equal in that 10 job applicants is twice as many as 5, a salary of $40,000 is twice as much as a salary of $20,000, and a desk six feet in length is twice as long as a desk that is three feet in length.

8

Now that you have some of the basics, the following chapters will provide information about particular types of statistics

Table 1.2
Applicant List for the Blue Moon Detective Agency

Rank	Applicant	Score
1	Maddie Hayes	99
2	David Addison	94
3	Tom Magnum	93
4	John Shaft	89
5	Frank Cannon	88
6	Thomas Banacek	87
7	Nora Charles	80
8	Joe Mannix	75
9	Jessica Fletcher	71

2. Statistics That Describe Data

IMAGINE THAT YOU are reading a technical report or a journal article and the author states, "As you can see from Table 2.01, our employees are well paid." As you glance at Table 2.01, you realize that the table contains raw data and is difficult to interpret. Because looking at raw data is not particularly meaningful, the first step in a statistical analysis is to summarize the raw data into a form that is meaningful. This initial summarization is called descriptive statistics and generally includes the sample size, a measure of central tendency, and a measure of dispersion.

Table 2.01
Raw Salary Data

Employee	Hourly Rate
Jim	$12.35
Ryan	$13.37
Pam	$12.35
Dwight	$13.11
Michael	$12.10
Oscar	$14.05
Kevin	$13.80

Sample Size

An important element in interpreting the value of a piece of research is the sample size—the number of participants included in a particular study. The number of participants may include an entire population (e.g., all employees at the Pulaski Furniture Plant) but more than likely represents a sample (100 students from Radford University) of a larger population (all college students in the United States). In most journal or technical reports, the number of people in a sample is denoted by the letter "N" and the number of people in a sub-sample (e.g., number of men, number of women) is denoted by a lower-case "n."

Research results derived from studies conducted with a small number of individuals should be interpreted with a lower degree of confidence than a study conducted with a large number of participants. It is important to note, however, that we also need to be aware of the difference between a small sample size and a small population. We remember being at a conference when one of the audience members questioned the accuracy of a presenter's results, because the sample size was only 25 participants. The speaker paused for a moment and then told the audience member that the 25 participants represented everyone in his police department, that is, the entire population. The interesting part of this story is that the audience member continued to comment that the use of 25 participants was still not acceptable. What the audience member failed to understand is that, although large samples are preferred over small samples, you can never acquire a sample size larger than the population available to you.

If a sample is used rather than an entire population, it is important to consider two aspects of the sample: the extent to which it is random and the extent to which it is representative of the population. In a *random sample*, every member of the population has an equal chance of being chosen for the sample. For example, suppose a large organization wants to determine the satisfaction level of its 3,000 employees. Because the budget for the project is not large enough to survey all 3,000 employees, the organization decides to sample 500 employees. To choose the 500, the organization might use a random numbers table or draw employee names from a hat. The more random the sample, the lower the sample size needed to generalize the results to the entire population.

Unfortunately in most research, the samples used are certainly not randomly selected. For example, suppose that a researcher at a university wants to study the relationship between employee personality and performance in a job interview. The population in this case would be every applicant in the world who has ever been on an employment interview. Ideally, the researcher would randomly sample from this population. However, as you can imagine, this would be impossible. So instead, the researcher might give a personality test to 250 applicants for positions at a local manufacturer and then try to generalize the results to other applicants. These 250 applicants would be called a *convenience sample*. Because the convenience samples used in most studies are drawn from one organization (e.g., municipal employees for the City of Mobile, Alabama) located in one region (e.g., south) of one country (e.g., U.S.), caution should be taken in generalizing the results to other organizations or cultures.

Convenience samples are fine as long as two conditions are met. The first is that the convenience sample must be similar to the population to which you want to apply your results. That is, the affirmative action opinions of 18 year-old college females in Alabama may not generalize to 50 year-old male factory workers in Ohio.

The second condition is that members of the convenience sample must be *randomly assigned* to the various research groups. Take for example a researcher wanting to study the effects of a training program on employee productivity. Before spending $100,000 training all 500 employees in the plant, the researcher might take a convenience sample (30 employees on the night shift) and randomly assign 15 to receive training (experimental group) and 15 to not receive training (control group). The subsequent job performance of the two groups can then be compared.

A sample is considered to be *representative* of the population if it is similar to the population in such important characteristics as sex, race, and age. Random samples are typically also representative samples. If a sample is not random, it is important to compare the percentage of women, minorities, older people, and other variables of interest to the percentages in the relevant population. If the sample differs from the population, it is difficult to generalize the finding of the study.

Although in most cases it is important to have a representative sample, there are times when it is necessary to

over-sample certain types of employees. A good example of
such a situation might be an employee attitude survey at an
organization in which only 10% of the employees are women. If
a random sample of 20 employees were drawn from a
population of 200, only two women would be in the sample, not
enough to compare the attitudes of women to men. To ensure
that gender differences in attitudes could be investigated, one
might randomly select 10 of the 180 men and 10 of the 20
women.

Measures of Central Tendency

Sets of statistics that describe a set of raw data are collectively
referred to as measures of central tendency. Individually, they
are referred to as the mean, median, and mode.

THE MEAN

The mean represents the mathematical average of a set of
data. To compute the mean, you sum all of the scores obtained
from your participants and then divide this sum by the total
number of participants. For example, as you can see in Table
2.02, the mean salary from the raw data first presented in
Table 2.01 is $13.02.

Table 2.02
Computing the Mean Salary

Employee	Hourly Rate
Michael	$12.10
Jim	$12.35
Pam	$12.35
Dwight	$13.11
Ryan	$13.37
Kevin	$13.80
Oscar	$14.05
Sum	91.14
N	7
Mean	$13.02

As you read journal articles and technical reports, you will find that M and $\bar{X}$ are the symbols most often used to represent the mean. Throughout this chapter, we will represent the mean with the symbol M.

THE MEDIAN

The median (M_d) is the point in your data where 50% of your raw scores fall above and 50% of your raw scores fall below. To determine the median, you begin by ranking your raw scores from highest to lowest and then find the score that falls in the middle. Using the data from the seven employees in Table 2.02, we see that the median would be $13.11, because three salaries ($12.10, $12.35, and $12.35) are lower than $13.11 and three salaries ($13.37, $13.80, and $14.06) are higher.

In our example, the median was easy to compute because there was an odd number of scores (7). When there is an even number of scores, you take the score that would theoretically fall between the two middle scores. As an example, let's add one more salary to our data set ($13.27):

$12.10, $12.35, $12.35, $13.11, $13.27, $13.37, $13.80, $14.06

When you count up from the lowest salary, the fourth salary is $13.11, and if you count down from the highest salary, the fourth salary is $13.27. To obtain the median salary, we would add the $13.11 and the $13.27 and divide by two. Thus the median salary would be $13.19. This is the point at which 50% of the salaries would fall above and 50% of the salaries would fall below, even though the salary of $13.19 is not an actual member of the data set.

THE MODE

The Mode (M_o) represents the most frequently occurring score in a set of data. Looking at our original sample data set in Table 2.02, $12.35 would be the mode as it occurs twice; whereas, each of the other salaries occurs only once. In the case where you have more than one score occurring multiple times (e.g. 16, 14, 13, 13, 10, 8, 7, 5, and 5), the data would be said to be bi-modal (having two modes: 13 and 5).

DECIDING WHICH CENTRAL TENDENCY MEASURE TO USE

Because there are three measures of central tendency (mean, median, mode), it is reasonable to ask which of the three is the "best" to use. With large sample sizes, the mean is the desired measure of the central tendency. With smaller sample sizes, however, the mean can be unduly influenced by an outlier—a score that is very different from the other scores. Thus, with smaller samples, the median should probably be used. Unfortunately, there is no real rule-of-thumb for what constitutes a "small sample;" and thus, the use of the mean or median is subject to personal preference.

To see how an outlier can affect the mean, look at Table 2.03. In Sample 1, the cognitive ability scores are relatively similar and the mean and the median are the same. In Sample 2, however, the cognitive ability score of 44—the outlier—is very different from the other scores, causing the mean to be much higher than the median. If we had 100 employees instead of the 7 in the example, the effect of one outlier would not result in the mean and the median being substantially different from one another.

Why would this matter? Suppose that you have just conducted a salary survey with the goal of adjusting your salaries to match the "industry standard." Your survey indicates a mean salary of $26,000 and a median salary of $22,000. If your organization is currently paying $24,000, use of the mean would suggest your employees are underpaid; whereas, use of the median would suggest that they are overpaid.

The mode should be used when the goal of the analysis is to determine the most likely event that will occur. For example, if a district attorney and a defense attorney were trying to reach a plea agreement, the defense attorney would probably be most interested in the sentence most commonly administered by a particular judge (mode) than the mean or median sentence.

Table 2.03
Cognitive Ability Scores for Two Samples

	Sample 1	Sample 2
	17	17
	18	18
	19	19
	20	20
	21	21
	22	22
	23	44
Mean	20	23
Median	20	20

Measures of Variability

Though measures of central tendency provide useful information regarding the "typical" score in a data set, they do not provide information about the distribution of scores. In fact, two data sets can have the same mean but also have very different distributions. Take for example the three distributions shown in Table 2.04. All three have a mean and median of 4.0, yet all of the day shift scores are the same (4), the night shift scores range from 3 to 5, and the evening shift scores range from 2 to 6. Measures of variability or dispersion are useful for determining the similarity of scores in a data set.

Table 2.04
Example of Three Distributions

	Day Shift	Evening Shift	Night Shift
	4	2	3
	4	3	3
	4	4	4
	4	5	5
	4	6	5
Mean	4	4	4

Table 2.05
Sample Performance Appraisal Ratings

Geller	Tribbiani
3	2
3	2
3	3
3	3
3	4
3	4

Let's use the performance appraisal data shown in Table 2.05 to demonstrate why we might care about measures of dispersion. Imagine that supervisors in River City rate their employees' performance on a five-point scale. A rating of 1 is terrible, 2 is needs improvement, 3 is satisfactory, 4 is good, and 5 is excellent. As the department head, you are pleased to see that the mean employee rating given by your two supervisors is 3.0, a number indicating that the typical employee was rated as satisfactory. However, in looking at the ratings, you notice that one of your supervisors rated every employee as performing at a satisfactory level (3); whereas, another supervisor assigned a rating of 2 to two employees, a rating of 3 to two employees, and a rating of 4 to two employees. The lack of dispersion in Geller's ratings and the use of only 3 of the 5 scale points by Tribbiani indicate either that the rating scale has too many points or that the supervisors did not properly evaluate their employees.

The most common measures of dispersion are the range, variance, and standard deviation.

RANGE

The range of a data set represents the spread of the data from the highest to the lowest score. To obtain the range, the highest score in the data set is subtracted from the lowest score. If we use Tribbiani's performance ratings from Table 2.05, the range is calculated by taking 4 (highest score) and subtracting 2 (lowest score). The range in performance ratings would be 2. Notice that our range does not include two of the points (1, 5) on the performance appraisal scale described in the previous paragraph. When reporting the range in a technical report, it is a good idea to list the lowest and highest scores obtained as well as the lowest and highest possible scores. For example, as you can see in Table 2.05, even though River City designed its performance appraisal ratings with a 5-point scale, in reality it has a 3-point scale.

STANDARD DEVIATION

The standard deviation is a statistic that, when combined with the mean, provides a range in which most scores in a distribution would fall. The standard deviation is based on something called the "normal curve" or the "bell curve." The idea behind the normal curve is that if the entire population was measured on something (e.g., intelligence, height), most people would score near the mean (the middle of the distribution) and very few would score considerably above or below the mean.

There are two ways that a standard deviation can be used to interpret data. The first is to focus on what the standard deviation tells us about a distribution. In viewing the normal curve, we find that 68.26% of scores fall within one standard deviation of the mean, 95.44% fall within two standard deviations of the mean, and 99.73% fall within three standard deviations of the mean. Let's use an example to demonstrate why this knowledge is useful.

Suppose that you are a trainer and will be training one group of employees in the morning and another in the afternoon. Prior to starting your training, you look at the IQ scores of the employees to be trained. As shown in Table 2.06, you are pleased that the employees in both classes have a mean IQ of 100. Given that a score of 100 is the average IQ in the U.S., you feel comfortable that your trainees will be bright enough to learn the material. However, as you look at the standard deviations, you realize that your afternoon class will be a trainer's nightmare.

Table 2.06
IQ Scores for Two Training Groups

Group	Mean IQ	SD	1 SD Range	2 SD Range
Morning	100	3	97 – 103	94 – 106
Afternoon	100	15	85 – 115	70 – 130

In the morning class, the standard deviation of 3 tells you that the IQ of 68% of your trainees is within 6 points of one another and that the IQ of 95% of your trainees is within 12 points of one another. In other words, the employees in the morning section have similar IQ levels. The afternoon class is a different matter. Though the average IQ is 100, the standard deviation is 15. Some of your trainees are so bright (e.g., IQ of 130) that they probably will be bored; whereas, others have such a low IQ (e.g., 70) that they will need remedial work. With such a large dispersion of IQs in the class, there is no way you could use the same material and the same pace to effectively train each employee. This is a conclusion that could not have been made with the mean alone.

The second way to use a standard deviation is to focus on what the standard deviation tells us about a particular score. For example, consider a salary survey for police officers reporting a mean salary of $25,000 and a standard deviation of $3,000. From this information we would know that about two-thirds (68.26%) of police departments pay their officers between $22,000 (the mean of $25,000 minus the standard deviation of $3,000) and $28,000 (the mean of $25,000 plus the standard deviation of $3,000). On the basis of these figures, we might note that although the $24,000 salary we pay is below the mean, the fact that it is within one standard deviation of the mean indicates our salary is not extremely low.

As another example, suppose that an applicant's score on an exam is one standard deviation above the mean. Using a chart such as that shown in Table 2.07, we see that the applicant's score was equal to or higher than 84.13% of the other applicants.

Now that we have discussed the usefulness of interpreting a standard deviation, it is time for some bad news. Inferences from a standard deviation will only be accurate if your data set is fairly large and your data are normally distributed (i.e., a plot of your data would look like a normal curve). Unfortunately, this is seldom the case. Though most measures are normally distributed in the world population, seldom are they normally distributed in any given organization or job. That is, because we screen out applicants with low ability and promote those with high ability, test scores and performance evaluations seldom resemble a normal curve.

Why does this matter? Consider the data shown in Table 2.08. The table shows the number of traffic citations written by police officers in two departments. The number of citations written in Elmwood approximates a normal distribution, whereas, the number written in Oakdale does not. As you can see from the table, the large standard deviation caused by a lack of a normal distribution in the Oakdale data would cause us to make the inference that an officer who is two standard deviations below the mean would be writing a negative number of tickets!

Table 2.07
Interpreting Standard Deviations

Standard Deviation	Cumulative %
- 3.0	0.14
- 2.0	2.28
- 1.5	6.68
- 1.0	15.87
- 0.5	30.85
0.0	50.00
+ 0.5	69.15
+ 1.0	84.13
+ 1.5	93.32
+ 2.0	97.72
+ 3.0	99.86

Table 2.08
Number of Traffic Citations Written

Officer	Police Department	
	Elmwood	Oakdale
A	1	1
B	2	1
C	2	1
D	3	1
E	3	1
F	3	1
G	4	1
H	4	1
I	4	1
J	4	1
K	5	1
L	5	1
M	5	1
N	5	9
O	5	9
P	5	9
Q	6	9
R	6	9
S	6	9
T	6	9
U	7	9
V	7	9
W	7	9
X	8	9
Y	8	9
Z	9	9
Mean	5.00	5.00
Standard deviation	2.00	4.08
1 SD Range	3 – 7	.92 – 9.08
2 SD Range	1 – 9	- 3.16 – 13.16

VARIANCE

A third measure of dispersion is the variance, which is simply the square of the standard deviation. Although the variance is important because it serves as the computational basis for several statistical analyses (e.g., *t*-tests, analysis of variance), by itself it serves no useful interpretative purpose. Thus, the standard deviation is more commonly reported in journal articles and technical reports than is the variance.

Standard Scores

Standard scores convert raw scores into a format that tells us the relationship of the raw score to the raw scores of others. They are useful because they allow us to better interpret and compare raw data collected on different measures. That is, suppose your daughter told you that she scored a 43 on the National History Test that was administered at school. With only that raw score, you wouldn't know whether to reward her by buying the new Britney Spears CD or punish her by making her listen to your Barry Manilow collection. However, if she told you that her score of 43 put her in the top 5%, your decision would be much easier.

To make raw scores more useful, we often convert them into something that by itself has meaning. Perhaps the simplest attempt at doing this is to convert a raw score into a percentage. For example, your daughter's history test score of 43 would be divided by the number of points possible (45) resulting in a score of 95.6%. However, the problem with percentages it that they don't tell us how everyone else scored. That is, a test might be so easy that a 95.6% is the lowest score in the class. Likewise, I remember taking a physiological psychology course as an undergraduate in which the best student in the class had an average of 58% across four tests!

The two most commonly used standard scores are *percentiles* and *Z-scores*.

PERCENTILES

A percentile is a score that indicates the percentage of people that scored at or below a certain score. For example, a salary survey might reveal that a salary of $26,000 is at the 71st percentile, indicating that 71% of the organizations surveyed pay $26,000 or less and 29% pay more than $26,000. Likewise, a student's score of 960 on the SAT might indicate that he scored at the 45th percentile—45% of the students scored at or below 960 and 55% scored higher. Because there are several formulas for determining percentiles, software programs such as Excel and SPSS often will arrive at different percentiles for the same set of data. We will discuss the method that is easiest to calculate and interpret.

As shown in Table 2.09, percentiles are computed by first ranking the raw scores from bottom to top. Then, the rank associated with each score is divided by the total number of scores, resulting in the percentile for the score. Notice that the highest score will always be at the 99th percentile; there is never a 100th percentile. The 25th percentile is also called the first quartile (Q1) and the 75th percentile is also called the third quartile (Q3).

Though some authors have written that the 50th percentile and the median are the same, this is not usually the case. Remember that by definition, the median is the point at which 50% of the scores fall below and 50% fall above. The 50th percentile, however, is the point at which 50% of the scores fall *at or below*. For example, if you have 6 scores with no ties (e.g., 20, 22, 24, 26, 28, 30), the 50th percentile would be the third highest score (24), whereas the median would be 25 as it falls between the third highest (24) and fourth highest (26) scores.

Table 2.09
Using Percentiles in a Salary Survey

Hourly Wage	Rank	Computation	Percentile
$32.17	20	20/20	99
$30.43	19	19/20	95
$28.72	18	18/20	90
$25.25	17	17/20	85
$24.96	16	16/20	80
$24.48	15	15/20	75
$22.92	14	14/20	70
$22.75	13	13/20	65
$22.11	12	12/20	60
$21.03	11	11/20	55
$20.86	10	10/20	50
$20.79	9	9/20	45
$20.35	8	8/20	40
$20.22	7	7/20	35
$20.03	6	6/20	30
$18.93	5	5/20	25
$16.65	4	4/20	20
$16.50	3	3/30	15
$16.25	2	2/20	10
$14.24	1	1/20	5

Z-Scores

Whereas percentiles are based on the actual distribution of scores in a data set (e.g., the salaries you obtained in your salary survey), z-scores use the mean and standard deviation of a set of scores to project where a score would fall in a normal distribution. When a data set is large and is normally distributed, percentiles and z-scores will yield similar interpretations.

To obtain a z-score for any given raw score, the following formula is used:

$$z = (\text{raw score} - \text{mean score}) \div \text{standard deviation}$$

25

For example, if you scored 70 on a test that has a mean of 60 and a standard deviation of 20, your z-score would be:

$z = (70 - 60) \div 20$
$z = 10 \div 20$
$z = 0.5$

A positive z-score indicates an above average score, whereas a negative z-score indicates a below average score. An average score would have a z of zero. In the previous example, our z-score of .5 indicates that our raw score of 70 is ½ a standard deviation (.5) above the mean. As shown in Table 2.10, a z-score of .5 would mean that our raw score of 70 is higher than the scores of 69.15% of the population.

Table 2.10
Interpreting Z-Scores

z-Score	% falling at or below score
- 3.00	0.14
- 2.00	2.28
- 1.75	4.01
- 1.50	6.68
- 1.25	10.56
- 1.00	15.87
- 0.75	22.66
- 0.50	30.85
- 0.25	40.13
0.00	50.00
+ 0.25	59.87
+ 0.50	69.15
+ 0.75	77.34
+ 1.00	84.13
+ 1.25	89.44
+ 1.50	93.32
+ 1.75	95.99
+ 2.00	97.72
+ 3.00	99.86

OTHER STANDARD SCORES

Because many people do not like working with negative values, they choose to use a standard score format other than the z-score. For example, the Minnesota Multiphasic Personality Inventory (MMPI) and the California Psychological Inventory (CPI) use a T-score in which the standardized mean for each scale is 50 and the standard deviation is 10. Thus, with z-scores, a person scoring one standard deviation below the mean would have a standard score of -1.00; whereas, with T scores, a person scoring one standard deviation below the mean would have a standard score of 40 (mean of 50 – one standard deviation of 10). As shown in Table 2.11, other examples include the College Entrance Examination Board (CEEB) scores used with the SAT and GRE that have a mean of 500 and a standard deviation of 100 and IQ scores that have a mean of 100 and a standard deviation of 15.

DECIDING WHICH STANDARD SCORE TO USE

Now that we have discussed percentiles, z-scores, and other standard scores, an important question becomes, "Which is best?" As with many questions like this, the answer depends on what you are trying to accomplish.

Percentiles are best when the person reading your analysis is not statistically inclined. Percentiles are also best when you are describing a specific data set that will not be generalized to other organizations. For example, suppose that you were conducting a study to determine which of your employees were "out of line" in terms of days absent or which of your police officers were "out of line" in the number of traffic citations they issued. Creating a percentile chart would probably result in a more accurate interpretation than would the use of z-scores.

Z-scores are best when standardizing scores for the purpose of conducting certain statistical analyses. In fact, it would be inappropriate to use percentiles for such a purpose. Converting z-scores to T-scores is best when your audience consists of people who are used to using tests such as the MMPI (e.g., clinical psychologists).

27

Table 2.11
Comparison of Standard Scores

Percentile		0.14	2.28	15.87	50.00	84.13	97.72	99.86	
Z score	- 4	- 3	- 2	- 1	0	+1	+2	+3	+4
T-Score	10	20	30	40	50	60	70	80	90
CEEB Score		200	300	400	500	600	700	800	
IQ	40	55	70	85	100	115	130	145	160

Statistical Symbols

Authors of journal articles and technical reports seldom include such terms as standard deviation or mean in their tables. Instead, they use symbols to represent their statistics. Table 2.12 contains the statistical symbols you are most likely to encounter in journal articles and technical reports that denote the statistics discussed in this chapter.

Table 2.12
Symbols Used to Denote Descriptive Statistics

Statistic	Common Symbols
Number of people	
In the sample (sample size)	N
In a sub-sample	n
Number of groups	K
Mean	$\underline{M}$, M, $\bar{X}$, M_x
Median	Mdn, M_d
Mode	Mo
Standard deviation	
Sample standard deviation	SD, s, Std Dev
Population standard deviation	σ
Variance	
Sample variance	s^2
Population variance	σ^2
Standard score	z
Quartile	
First quartile	$Q1$
Third quartile	$Q3$

Applying Your Knowledge

You can apply what you have learned in this chapter by reading the following articles in *Applied H.R.M. Research* (www.radford.edu/~applyhrm) and in *Public Personnel Management*.

Buttigieg, S. (2005). Gender and race differences in scores on the Employee Aptitude Survey: Test 5 Space Visualization. *Applied H.R.M. Research, 10*(1), 45-46.

Kethley, R. B., & Terpstra, D. E. (2005). An analysis of litigation associated with the use of the application form in the selection process. *Public Personnel Management, 34*(4), 357-375.

Roberts, G. E. (2004). Municipal government benefits practices and personnel outcomes: Results from a national survey. *Public Personnel Management, 33*(1), 1-19.

Selden, S. C. (2005). Human resource management in American counties, 2002. *Public Personnel Management, 34*(1), 59-84.

3. Statistics That Test Differences Between Groups

A COMMONLY ASKED question in human resources is whether two or more groups differ on some variable. That is, do the average salaries of men and women differ? Are the average performance appraisal scores of minorities and non-minorities different? Which of five recruitment methods produces the greatest number of hires? The most commonly used statistics to answer these questions are the *t*-test, chi-square, analysis of variance (ANOVA), and Fisher's Exact Test. The statistic used is a function of the number of groups, the type of measurement, the number of independent variables, and the number of dependent variables.

Choosing the Right Statistical Test

Researchers typically are interested in testing the significance of differences between means, medians, or frequencies. A *t*-test or ANOVA is used to test differences in means, a Fisher's Exact Test is used to test differences in medians, and a chi-square is used to test differences in frequencies.

TESTING DIFFERENCES IN MEANS

Three factors are used to determine if differences between means are statistically significant: size of the difference betweens the means, the sample size, and the variability of scores within each group being compared. The greater the difference in means, the greater the sample size; and the lower the variability of scores within groups, the greater the chance of two means being statistically different from one another. For example, if data from 500 employees (large sample size) indicate there is a $15,000 difference between men's and women's salaries (large difference between means), the difference will probably be statistically significant. However, in a situation in which there is a $300 difference (small difference between means) in the salaries of 16 men and 10 women (small sample size), it is unlikely that the difference would be statistically significant. Although the large difference in means and the larger sample size probably makes sense, let's spend a moment discussing the variability issue.

As mentioned in Chapter 2, variability is the extent to which scores differ from one another. The statistics used to test group differences in means (e.g., t-test, ANOVA) compare the variability of scores within a group with the variability of scores between groups. For example, suppose we conduct a study in which we compare the number of hours per week that men and women spend watching ESPN. The results of our study are shown in Table 3.01. There is little variability in scores within each sex (i.e., the scores are similar), but there is much variability in scores between the groups. When such a situation occurs, the difference between the mean for men (5.13) and the mean for women (3.46) is likely to be statistically significant.

Table 3.01 Hours spent watching ESPN

Women			Men		
4	3	4	5	5	5
3	4	3	5	5	5
4	3	4	5	5	5
3	4	3	5	6	5
4	3	3	6	5	5

Table 3.02 Hours spent watching *Law and Order*

Women			Men		
5	2	1	5	9	4
0	1	3	8	5	9
1	7	4	1	0	4
10	6	3	10	2	7
3	4	2	2	1	10

A very different pattern occurs, however, in Table 3.02. Although the means for men and women are the same as they were in Table 3.01, the variability *within* each group is much greater. Whereas in Table 3.01, where the highest number of hours for women (4) is lower than the lowest number of hours for men (5), the highs and lows for men in Table 3.02 are the same as those for women. With such high variability, it is unlikely that the differences in means would be statistically significant.

Table 3.03: Statistics that test differences in means

Number of Independent Variables	Number of Dependent Variables	
	One	Two or more
One independent variable		
Two levels	t-test	MANOVA
Two or more levels	ANOVA	MANOVA
Two or more independent variables	ANOVA	MANOVA

In testing differences in means, *t*-tests and ANOVAs are the most commonly used statistics. As shown in Table 3.03, when there is only one independent variable (e.g., sex *or* race) with only two levels (e.g., male, female or minority, nonminority), a *t*-test is used to test group differences in means. When there is one independent variable with more than two levels (e.g., race: African American, White, Hispanic American, and Asian American) or there are two or more independent variables (e.g., sex *and* race), an analysis of

33

variance (ANOVA) is used. When there are more than two dependent variables (e.g., turnover and absenteeism), a multivariate analysis of variance (MANOVA) is used.

For example, a *t*-test might be used to test differences in:

- Salary (1 dependent variable) between males and females—2 levels (male, female) of 1 independent variable (sex)

	Sex	
	Male	Female
Salary	$46,000	$43,000

- Assessment center scores (1 dependent variable) between minorities and non-minorities—2 levels (minority, non-minority) of 1 independent variable (minority status)

	Race	
	Nonminority	Minority
Assessment Center Score	52.6	47.3

- Job satisfaction levels (1 dependent variable) between clerical and production workers—2 levels (clerical, production) of 1 independent variable (job type).

	Job Type	
	Production	Clerical
Job Satisfaction Score	6.1	7.5

An analysis of variance (ANOVA) might be used to test differences in:

- Salary (1 dependent variable) among White, African American, and Hispanic employees—3 levels (White, African American, and Hispanic) of 1 independent variable (race).

		Race	
	White	African American	Hispanic
Salary	$44,000	$41,000	$41,500

- Salary (1 dependent variable) on the basis of race and gender (2 independent variables: race and gender)

		Race	
Gender	White	African American	Hispanic
Male	$44,000	$41,000	$41,500
Female	$42,000	$39,000	$40,000

TESTING DIFFERENCES IN MEDIANS

As stated in Chapter 2, medians are used instead of means when sample sizes are small or when there are outliers that might skew the data. To test the significance of difference in medians, Fisher's Exact Tests are used when sample sizes are small. The actual calculations for the Fisher's can get complicated and are beyond the scope of this book. However, let's discuss the basic concept behind such a test. As depicted in Table 3.04, assume that the median salary for a group of 12 police officers is $28,500. We are interested in determining if female officers are paid less than male officers. Because we have such a small number of employees (4 women, 8 men), we should not use a t-test to test differences in mean salaries for men and women. Instead, we can use the Fisher's Exact Test to test the difference in median salaries. As shown in Table 3.05, 25% of women have salaries above the department median and 75% have salaries below the median. For men, 62.5% (5/8) have salaries above the median and 37.5% (3/8) have salaries below the median. A Fischer's test would determine the probability that these differences are statistically significant (i.e., did not occur by chance).

35

Table 3.04
Salaries for a small police department

Salary	Officer Sex
$32,000	Female
$31,500	Male
$31,000	Male
$30,900	Male
$30,200	Male
$29,000	Male
$28,000	Female
$27,800	Male
$27,200	Male
$27,000	Female
$26,500	Female
$26,000	Male

Table 3.05
Number of men and women whose salary falls above and below the median

	Women	Men	
Above the median	1	5	6
Below the median	3	3	6
	4	8	12

TESTING DIFFERENCES IN FREQUENCIES

At times, a researcher wants to test differences in frequencies rather than differences in means or medians. For example, as shown in Table 3.06, an HR manager might want to see if the distribution of men and women across jobs is the same. Or, as shown in Table 3.07, the HR manger might want to determine whether there are differences in the number of people hired using different recruitment methods. In situations such as these, a chi-square is the most commonly used statistic.

Table 3.06		
Position Type	Male	Female
Management	15	5
Clerical	2	27
Production	45	13

Table 3.07	
Recruitment Method	Hired
Referral	43
Advertisement	27
Job Fair	26

Interpreting Statistical Results

t-TEST

When *t*-tests are used in technical reports or journal articles, the results of the analysis are typically listed in the following format:

$$t\,(45) = 2.31, p < .01$$

The number in the parentheses, in this case 45, represents the *degrees of freedom*. For a *t*-test, the degrees of freedom are the number of people in the sample minus 2. Thus, in our example above, our 45 degrees of freedom indicate that our *t*-test was conducted on scores from 47 people.

The next number, the 2.31, is the value of our *t*-test. The larger the *t*-value, the greater the difference in scores between the two groups. With sample sizes of 120 or more, the *t*-value can be interpreted as approximately the number of standard deviations in which the two groups differ. For example, a *t* of 2.0 would indicate that the salary for males is about 2 standard deviations higher than the salary for females. Likewise, a *t* of 1.5 would indicate a difference of approximately 1½ standard deviations. With sample sizes of less than 120, the interpretation of a *t* value is not as precise.

The *significance level* is indicated by the notation "$p <$ .01" with the .01 indicating that the probability of our results occurring by chance is 1 in 100 (.01). Traditionally, when a significance level is .05 or lower (e.g., .04, .02, .001), our results are considered to be "statistically significant." As shown in

37

Table 3.08, the significance level is a function of the *t*-value and the degrees of freedom. The higher the degrees of freedom (the greater the sample size), the lower the *t*-value needed to be considered statistically significant.

When reading the results of a *t*-test in a journal or technical report, you might find that the article mentioned one of three types of *t*-tests: One sample, two samples, or paired difference.

Table 3.08
t-value needed for statistical significance (two-tailed test)

Degrees of Freedom	Significance Level	
	.05	.01
10	2.228	3.169
15	2.131	2.947
20	2.086	2.845
30	2.042	2.750
40	2.021	2.704
60	2.000	2.660
120	1.980	2.617

A one-sample *t*-test is used when a researcher wants to compare the mean from a sample with a particular mean. For example, suppose that a police department found that the average number of complaints received for each officer was 1.3 per year. The national average for complaints is 1.2. A one-sample *t*-test could be used to determine if the rate of 1.3 for the town was statistically higher than the national rate of 1.2.

A two-sample *t*-test is used to compare the means of two independent groups. For example, a group of 30 employees received customer service training, and the town manager wants to compare the complaint rate for these employees with that of 40 employees who did not receive the training. Another example would be that a compensation manager found that the average salary for male police officers in the town was $32,200, and the average salary for female police officers was $30,800.

To determine if the average salary for men was statistically higher than the average salary for women, a two-sample t-test would be used.

A paired-difference t-test is used when you have two measures from the same sample. For example, police officers in one department averaged 1.3 complaints per officer. To reduce the number of complaints, the chief had each of the officers attend a training seminar on communication skills. In the year following the seminar, the average complaint rate for those *same* officers was 1.0. A paired-difference t-test would be used to determine if the decrease from 1.3 to 1.0 was statistically significant.

ANALYSIS OF VARIANCE – ONE INDEPENDENT VARIABLE

When the results of an ANOVA are reported in a technical report or journal, two tables are usually provided: a means table and a source table. The source table reports the results of the ANOVA, and the means table provides descriptive statistics that serve as the basis for the source table.

As shown in Table 3.09, the source table provides five pieces of statistical information, only three of which—degrees of freedom (df), F value (F), and the probability level ($p <$)—are important for interpreting the results of the ANOVA.

Degrees of Freedom

In an ANOVA source table, the degrees of freedom for an independent variable are the number of groups in the variable minus one. For example, as shown in Table 3.09, in the Education variable, there were three groups: high school diploma, associate's degree, and bachelor's degree. The degrees of freedom, then, would be 3 groups − 1 = 2 degrees of freedom. Had there been four education levels (i.e., high school diploma, associate's degree, bachelor's degree, master's degree), there would have been three degrees of freedom (4 education levels − 1 = 3).

The total degrees of freedom represent the number of people in our analysis minus one. The 673 total degrees of freedom in Table 3.09 indicate that our analysis was based on data from 674 employees (674 − 1 = 673 degrees of freedom).

F Statistic

An ANOVA with one independent variable will yield one F value. Statistically, the F value is computed by dividing the mean square (MS) for the variable by the mean square error. For example, the F of 35.32 for education was computed by dividing the mean square (MS) for education (3369.62) by the mean square error (95.40). An F of 1.0 or less indicates that the independent variable had the effect size that we would have expected by chance. An F value greater than 1 indicates that the effect of our variable was greater than what would be expected by chance. In the example shown in Table 3.09, the F of 35.32 for education indicates that the effect of education on academy grades is 35 times what would be expected by chance.

Significance Level

As with t-test results, the significance level of our F ratio is indicated by the notation, "$p < .0001$," indicating that the probability of our results occurring by chance is 1 in 10,000 (.0001). As mentioned earlier, a probability level less than .05 is considered "statistically significant." As you can see from Table 3.09, the effect for education is significant at the .0001 level. This level indicates that the main effect for education is statistically significant because it is less than .05.

As shown in Table 3.10, the significance of an F ratio is determined by the sample size and the number of levels in the independent variable. The greater the sample size, the lower the F ratio needed for statistical significance. As you can see from the table, we would need an F ratio of about 3 (2.99) for the effect of education on academy grades to be statistically significant. Our ratio of 35.32 greatly exceeds that value.

Table 3.09
Example of an ANOVA source table for one independent variable

Effect	df	SS	MS	F	$p <$
Education	2	6739.24	3369.62	35.32	.0001
Error	671	64011.83	95.40		
Total	673	70751.07			

If our F ratio is not statistically significant, we cannot conclude that our independent variable (e.g., education) had an effect on the dependent variable (e.g., academy grades). If our F ratio is significant, we have one more analysis to perform. Although the significant F ratio indicates that academy cadets performed differently on the basis of their education level, we don't know if academy performance differed for each of the three degree types. That is, it may be that cadets with associate's degrees or bachelor's degrees outperformed cadets with a high school diploma, but cadets with associate's degrees or bachelor's degrees performed at the same level. To get a clearer picture of which means differ from one another, *post-hoc* tests are conducted. Examples of such tests include Scheffe, Tukey, Duncan, LSD, and Newman-Keuls.

Table 3.10
Approximate F ratio needed for significance at the .05 level

Sample Size	Levels in the Independent Variable			
	2	3	4	5
10	5.12	4.46	4.35	4.53
20	4.38	3.55	3.20	3.01
30	4.18	3.34	2.96	2.74
60	4.00	3.15	2.76	2.52
100	3.94	3.09	2.70	2.46
200	3.89	3.04	2.65	2.41
Infinity	3.84	2.99	2.60	2.37

In journal articles and technical reports, the results of these tests are typically depicted using superscripts next to the mean. Means that share the same superscript are not statistically different from one another. For example, the three means in Table 3.11 have different superscripts, thus they are statistically different from each other. As shown in the examples in Table 3.12,

- In Example 1, cadets with bachelor's degrees and associate's degrees performed better than cadets with high school diplomas, but there was no difference between cadets with associate's degrees and bachelor's degrees.
- In Example 2, cadets with bachelor's degrees outperformed those with associate's degrees who outperformed those with high school diplomas.
- In Example 3, cadets with bachelor's degrees performed better than those with associate's degrees or high school diplomas. Cadets with associate's degrees did not outperform cadets with a high school diploma.

Table 3.11
Means Table

Education Level	Mean Academy Score	Standard Deviation
High school diploma	77.09[a]	10.83
Associate's degree	81.31[b]	9.09
Bachelor's degree	83.94[c]	8.25

Table 3.12
Examples of post-hoc test results

Education Level	Example 1	Example 2	Example 3
High school diploma	73.24[a]	73.24[a]	73.24[a]
Associate's degree	77.89[b]	77.89[b]	75.99[a]
Bachelor's degree	78.01[b]	80.21[c]	80.21[b]

ANALYSIS OF VARIANCE: TWO OR MORE INDEPENDENT VARIABLES

As shown in Table 3.13, an ANOVA produces an *F* value for each independent variable and combination of independent variables. Each individual variable is called a *main effect* and the combination of variables is called an *interaction*. When there are two independent variables, three outcomes are possible:

- One or both main effects are statistically significant but the interaction is not (Table 3.14)
- Neither main effect is significant but the interaction is (Table 3.15)
- One of the main effects is significant as is the interaction (Table 3.16)

A significant interaction indicates that the effect of one variable depends on the level of the other dependent variable. For example, as shown in Table 3.15, there are no significant differences in overall performance ratings between men and women or minorities and nonminorities. The significant interaction, however, tells us that sex and race interact so that white males and minority females are receiving the highest performance evaluations. To be sure of which means are different from one another, we would use one of the planned comparison tests previously mentioned.

Table 3.13

Example of an ANOVA source table for two independent variables

Effect	df	SS	MS	F	$p <$
Race	1	1.31708	1.31708	9.31	.003
Sex	1	0.00896	0.00896	0.06	.802
Sex * Race	1	0.51953	0.51953	3.67	.058
Error	107	15.13865	0.14148		
Total	110	16.98421			

Table 3.14
Example of significant main effect with no interaction

Source Table

Effect	df	SS	MS	F	*p* <
Race	1	.0073	.0073	14.09	.0006
Sex	1	0.5198	0.5198	0.20	.6593
Sex * Race	1	.0026	0.0026	0.07	.7937
Error	36	1.3279	0.0369		
Total	39	1.8576			

Means Table

Sex	White	Minority	
Male	2.42	2.46	2.44
Female	2.21	2.22	2.22
	2.31	2.34	2.33

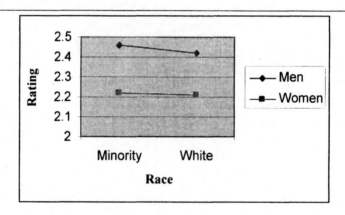

Table 3.15
Example of a significant interaction but no main effects

Source Table				
Effect	df	SS	MS	F	p <
Race	1	0.0172	0.0172	1.20	.2804
Sex	1	0.0056	0.0056	0.04	.8441
Sex * Race	1	0.2873	0.2873	20.03	.0001
Error	36	0.5162	0.0143		
Total	39	0.8213			

Means Table		
Sex	White	Minority	
Male	2.48	2.27	2.38
Female	2.30	2.43	2.43
	2.39	2.34	2.40

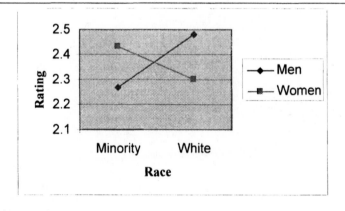

Table 3.16

Example of a significant interaction and main effects

Source Table				
Effect	df	SS	MS	F	p <
Race	1	0.2234	0.2234	5.64	.0230
Sex	1	0.5086	0.5086	12.83	.0010
Sex * Race	1	0.2576	0.2576	6.50	.0152
Error	36	1.4267	0.0396		
Total	39	2.4163			

Means Table		
Sex	White	Minority	
Male	2.59	2.28	2.44
Female	2.21	2.22	2.22
	2.40	2.25	2.33

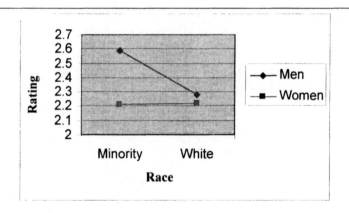

FISHER'S EXACT TEST

In the last few pages, we discussed how *t*-tests are used to test the difference between two means. To test the difference between two medians, a Fisher's Exact Test can be used. Interpreting a journal article or technical report using a

Fisher's is relatively easy because the results are usually reported in a manner such as, FET = .023. A value of .025 or lower is considered statistically significant at the .05 level and a value of .005 or lower is considered significant at the .01 level. Thus, the FET of .023 would be significant at the .05 level. An FET of .067 would not be statistically significant.

CHI-SQUARE

As mentioned previously, a chi-square is encountered in the literature when researchers want to tests differences in frequencies. In human resources, chi-square tests are often used to determine adverse impact. Whereas, the four-fifths rule is a rule-of-thumb to determine adverse impact, a chi-square analysis is a method to determine if differences are statistically significant. In journal articles, chi-square results are often reported in a manner such as, $\chi^2(2) = 2.69$, $p < .04$. The (2) is the degrees of freedom, the 2.69 is the chi-square value, and the .04 is the probability level.

With a chi-square analysis, the degrees of freedom are the number of groups minus one. For example, if the analysis examined racial frequencies (white, African American, Hispanic, Asian), the degrees of freedom would be three: four races minus one. In the example shown back in Table 3.07, the degrees of freedom would be two (three recruitment methods minus one). When the analysis involves two variables, such as that shown back in Table 3.06, the degrees of freedom are the number of groups in the first variable minus one, multiplied by the number of groups in the second variable minus one. The degrees of freedom for Table 3.06 would be two: (two for position type [3 positions minus 1] multiplied by one for sex [2 sexes minus one].)

The significance level is determined by the size of the chi-square value and the degrees of freedom. The greater the degrees of freedom, the higher the chi-square value needed for statistical significance. An example of the chi-square values needed for statistical significance is shown in Table 3.17. As

47

you can seen in the table, with 3 degrees of freedom, a chi-square value of 7.81 or higher is needed for a frequency distribution to be significantly different at the .05 level and 11.34 for the .01 level of significance.

It is important to understand that when there are more than two levels of a variable, a significant chi-square only indicates that the distribution of frequencies is not equal. Unlike the paired comparisons available for ANOVA, there is no test with chi-square to indicate which frequencies are different from one another. For example, in Table 3.06, a significant chi-square would tell us that males and females are not represented equally across positions; but we would not know which positions are statistically different from one another. In looking at the table we would probably make the assumption that males are represented more in the management and production positions and less often in the clerical positions; but we could not state this with statistical certainty.

Table 3.17
Chi-square valued needed for statistical significance

Degrees of Freedom	Probability Level	
	.05	.01
1	3.84	663
2	5.99	9.21
3	7.81	11.34
4	9.49	13.28
5	11.07	15.09
6	12.59	16.81
7	14.07	18.48
8	15.51	20.09
9	16.92	21.67
10	18.31	23.21
20	31.41	37.57
30	43.77	50.89

Applying Your Knowledge

You can apply what you have learned in this chapter by reading the following articles in *Applied H.R.M. Research* (www.radford.edu/~applyhrm) and in *Public Personnel Management*.

t-test

Barclay, L. A. & York, K. M. (2003). Clear logic and fuzzy guidance: A policy capturing study of merit raise decisions. *Public Personnel Management, 32*(2), 287-299.

Analysis of Variance (ANOVA)

Levine, S. P. & Feldman, R. S. (2002). Women and men's nonverbal behavior and self-monitoring in job interview setting. *Applied H.R.M. Research, 7*(1), 1-14.

Roberts, L. L., Konczak, L. J, & Macan, T. H. (2004). Effects of data collection methods on organizational climate survey results. *Applied H.R.M. Research, 9*(1), 13-26.

Chi-square

Lee, J.A., Havighurst, L.C., & Rassel, G. (2004). Factors related to court references to performance appraisal fairness and validity. *Public Personnel Management, 23*(1), 61-69.

4. Understanding Correlation

What is Correlation?

CORRELATION IS A statistical procedure that allows a researcher to determine the *relationship* between two variables. For example, we might want to know the relationship between an employment test and future employee performance, job satisfaction and job attendance, or education level and performance in a training program. Though correlations show the extent to which two variables are *related*, it is important to understand that correlational analysis does not necessarily say anything about whether one variable *causes* another.

Why does a correlation coefficient (the result of a correlational analysis) not indicate a cause and effect relationship? Because a third variable, an *intervening* variable, often accounts for the relationship between two variables. Take the example often used by psychologist David Schroeder. Suppose there is a very high correlation between the number of ice cream cones sold in New York during August and the number of babies that die during August in India. Does eating ice cream in New York kill babies in another nation? No, that would not make sense. Instead, we look for that third variable that would explain our high correlation. In this case, the answer is clearly the summer heat.

Another interesting example of an intervening variable was provided by psychologist Wayman Mullins in a conference presentation about the incorrect interpretation of correlation coefficients. Mullins pointed out that data show a strong negative correlation between the number of cows per square mile and the crime rate. With his tongue firmly planted in his cheek, Mullins suggested that New York City could rid itself of crime by importing millions of head of cattle. Of course, the real interpretation for the negative correlation is that crime is greater in urban areas than in rural areas.

As shown above, a good researcher should always be cautious about variables that seem related. Several years ago, *People* magazine reported on a minister who conducted a "study" of 500 pregnant teenage girls and found that rock music was being played when 450 of them became pregnant. The minister concluded that because the two factors are related (that is, they occurred at the same time), rock music must cause pregnancy. His solution? Outlaw rock music, and teenage pregnancy would disappear. However, suppose we found that in all 500 cases of teenage pregnancy, a pillow was also present. By using the same logic as the minister, the real solution would be to outlaw pillows, not rock music. Although both "solutions" are certainly strange, the point should be clear: just because two events occur at the same time or seem to be related does not mean that one event or variable causes another.

Interpreting a Correlation Coefficient

MAGNITUDE AND DIRECTION

The result of correlational analysis is a number called a correlation coefficient. The values of this coefficient range from 0 to +1 and from 0 to -1. The further the coefficient is from zero, the greater the relationship between two variables. That is, a correlation of .40 shows a stronger relationship between two variables than does a correlation of .20. Likewise, a correlation of -.39 shows a stronger relationship than a correlation of +.30 because, even though the -.39 is negative, it is further from zero than the +.30.

The + and - signs indicate the *direction* of the correlation. A positive (+) correlation means that as the values of one variable increase, the values of a second variable also increase. For example, we might find a positive correlation between intelligence and scores on a classroom exam. This would mean that the more intelligent the student, the higher his or her score on the exam.

A negative (-) correlation means that as the values of one variable increase, the values of a second variable decrease. For example, we would probably find a negative correlation between the number of beers students drink the night before a test and their scores on that test. As the number of beers increases, their test scores are likely to decrease. In human resources, we find negative correlations between job satisfaction and absenteeism and between nervousness and interview success.

Though correlation coefficients are computed using a statistical formula, they are most easily understood through scatter plots such as those found in Figures 4.1, 4.2, and 4.3. Each of these figures depicts the scores of 12 applicants on an employment test and their supervisor ratings after 6 months on the job. Figure 4.1 shows how the scatter plot would look if test scores and performance ratings had a high positive correlation, Figure 4.2 shows a plot of a negative correlation, and Figure 4.3 shows a plot of two uncorrelated variables.

To interpret a scatter plot, use the rule-of-thumb taught by psychologist Tom Pierce. Count the number of people falling in quadrants C and B and then count the number falling in quadrants A and D. If the number in quadrants C and B is higher than in A and D, there is a positive correlation: the greater the difference in numbers, the stronger the correlation. Note in Figure 4.1 there are nine points in quadrants B and C and only three in quadrants A and D. If the number in quadrants A and D is higher than in C and B, there is a negative correlation. Note in Figure 4.2 there are eight points

Figure 4.1
Example of a Positive Correlation

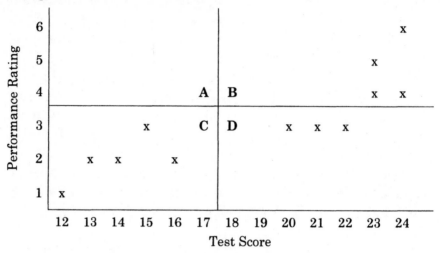

Figure 4.2
Example of a Negative Correlation

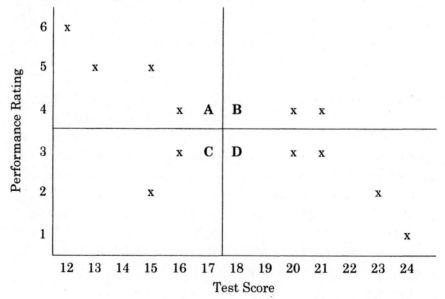

Figure 4.3
Example of Two Uncorrelated Variables

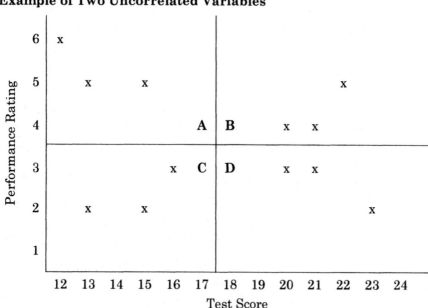

in quadrants A and D and only four in quadrants C and B. If the number is the same, there is no correlation. Note in Figure 4.3 that there are six points in quadrants A and D and six in quadrants C and B.

Factors Limiting the Magnitude of a Correlation

Suppose we know the "real" relationship between cognitive ability and performance in the police academy is .60, yet in our own study, we obtained a correlation of .40. What would explain this discrepancy? Probably three factors: *test unreliability, criterion unreliability,* and *range restriction.*

Reliability. The size of a correlation coefficient is limited by the reliability of the two variables being correlated (reliability is the extent to which a score is free from error). So, if our two measures (in this case, scores on a cognitive ability test and grades in the academy) have low reliability, the correlation between the test scores and academy grades (our validity coefficient) will be lower than expected. There are four types of reliability: test-retest, alternate-forms, internal, and scorer.

With *test-retest reliability*, people take the same test twice. The scores from the first administration of the test are correlated with scores from the second to determine whether they are similar. If they are, the test is said to have *temporal stability*: the test scores are stable across time and not highly susceptible to such random daily conditions as illness, fatigue, stress, or uncomfortable testing conditions.

With *alternative-forms reliability*, two forms of the same test are constructed. The scores on the two forms are then correlated to determine whether they are similar. If they are, the test is said to have *form stability*. Multiple forms of a test are common in situations in which individuals might take the test more than once (e.g., a promotion exam) or when there is concern that test takers will copy answers from another test taker.

With *internal reliability*, the similarity of responses to test items is compared. In a test with high internal reliability, we would expect a test taker to answer similar items in a similar way. That is, we would expect a person who rates the item "I am outgoing" as being similar to them would also rate the item "I like to talk with people" as also being similar to them. Measures of internal reliability that you might encounter in a journal article include split-half reliability, Cronbach's coefficient alpha, and the Kuder-Richardson Formula 10 (K-R 20).

Scorer reliability is the extent to which two people scoring a test will obtain the same test score. Scorer reliability is an issue especially in projective or subjective tests (e.g., the Rorschach Ink Blot Test, interviews, writing samples) in which there is no one correct answer, but even tests scored with the use of keys suffer from scorer mistakes. For example, Allard, Butler, Faust, and Shea (1995) found that 53% of hand-scored personality tests contained at least one scoring error and that 19% contained enough errors to alter a clinical diagnosis. When human judgment of performance is involved, scorer reliability is discussed in terms of interrater reliability. That is, will two interviewers give an applicant similar ratings, or will two supervisors give an employee similar performance ratings?

Range Restriction. A correlation coefficient is also limited by the range of test scores and performance measures that are included in the study—the wider the range of scores, the higher the validity coefficient (the correlation between a test score and a measure of job performance). Unfortunately, in the typical validity study in which we correlate a test with some measure of performance, we usually encounter something called *range restriction*. That is, we don't have a full range of test scores or performance ratings. For example, in a given employment situation, few employees are at the extremes of a performance scale. Employees who would be at the bottom were either never hired or have since been terminated. Employees at the upper end of the performance scale either got promoted or went to an organization that paid more money.

Range restriction is important because it is easiest to predict the future performance of people with extremely high or extremely low test scores. For example, suppose that 10 students scored 1400 on the GRE and another 10 scored 700. Most people would be willing to bet that most of the students with a score of 1400 will do better in graduate school than most of the students with a score of 700. However, suppose that one student scores 900 and another scored 910. How many people would be willing to bet the mortgage on such a small difference in points?

Curvilinearity. Another problem that can lower the size of a correlation coefficient is *curvilinearity*. As depicted in Figure 4.4, one of the assumptions behind correlation is that the two variables being correlated are linearly related—the scores on

57

one variable are related in a straight line to scores on the other variable.

Figure 4.4
Example of a Linear Relationship

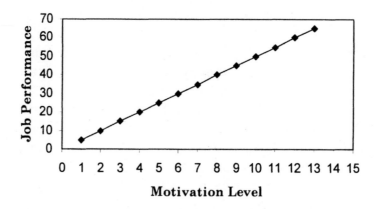

However, many things in life are not linearly related. For example, research strongly indicates that bright people perform better than less bright people in the police academy. But, is there a point at which increases in intelligence don't help? In the example shown in Figure 4.5, academy performance increases as IQ scores increase until we reach an IQ of 110. After scores of 110, increasing amounts of IQ do not result in better performance. Why would we obtain such a relationship? Because the material learned in the academy is only so difficult; and at some point, being super smart may not provide any advantage over being smart.

In human resources, we see a similar relationship between years of experience and job performance. That is, the difference in the job performance of a person with two years experience versus a person with no experience or with one year experience is probably fairly great. However, after ten years, would an employee with 15 years of experience perform better than an employee with 12 years of experience?

Figure 4.5
Example of a Curvilinear Relationship

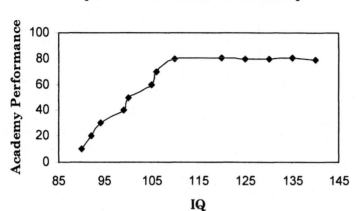

Curvilinearity also occurs in situations in which too little or too much of a variable could actually result in decreased performance—something called the "inverted U" that is depicted in Figure 4.6 The relationship between arousal and performance provides the perfect example. A person who has very low levels of arousal is probably not motivated enough to do well on a task. A person with very high levels of arousal will become nervous and perform poorly. However, a person with a moderate level of arousal has enough energy to be motivated but not so much that performance will decrease (too nervous and uptight). So, even though there is a relationship between arousal and performance, the relationship is not linear. Thus, a simple correlation between arousal levels and performance would probably not result in a significant correlation, and we would incorrectly conclude that there is no correlation between the two variables. Fortunately, there are some statistical adjustments that we can make to test for this possibility (converting our measures to z-scores and then squaring them). Just as fortunately, such adjustments are beyond the scope of this chapter—and probably your interest as well!

Figure 4.6
Example of the "Inverted U"

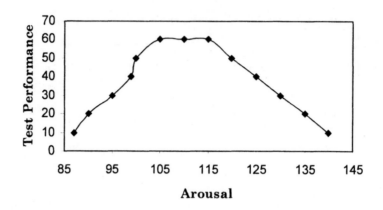

An interesting example of the "inverted U" was provided in 1996 by the New London, Connecticut police department. New London required that applicants score between 20 and 27 on the Wonderlic Personnel Test (a cognitive ability test), reasoning that people scoring below 20 were too dumb to be cops, and those scoring above 27 were too smart and would be bored performing the day-to-day law enforcement duties. Though New London had no statistical proof to back their claim, the 2nd Circuit Court of Appeals upheld the city's practice of not hiring applicants who were too bright (*Jordan v. City of New London*, 2000). As you can imagine, New London received lots of bad publicity and a good deal of ribbing from other cities. The San Francisco Police Department went so far as to hold a press conference inviting these "too smart applicants" rejected by New London to move out west and apply for the SFPD!

STATISTICAL SIGNIFICANCE

To determine if we are even allowed to interpret a correlation coefficient, we must first compute something called a significance level (see Chapter 1 for a discussion of significance levels). Significance levels tell us the probability that our correlation coefficient occurred by chance alone. That is, if we obtain a correlation of .30 between a test score and supervisor ratings of on-the-job performance, is there really a relationship between the two variables or is our correlation a chance finding?

The significance level for a correlation coefficient is a function of two factors: the size of the correlation coefficient and the sample size used in the study. The greater the sample size, the smaller the correlation needed for statistical significance. For example, as shown in Table 4.1, a correlation of .19 would be significant if we had 100 employees in our study but not if we had only 50 employees.

Table 4.1
Sample sizes needed for statistical significance

Sample Size	Smallest Significant Correlation (p < .05)
10	.63
20	.44
30	.36
40	.31
50	.27
60	.25
70	.23
80	.22
90	.21
100	.19

If a correlation coefficient is not statistically significant, we cannot try to interpret it as being high/low or useful/not useful. We essentially pretend that it doesn't exist. If, however, the correlation is statistically significant, we must address the issue of practical significance. A good example of this need to separately consider statistical and practical significance comes from the case of *Lanning v. Southeastern Pennsylvania Transportation Authority* (3rd Cir, June 29, 1999).

In trying to justify its use of a physical agility test, SEPTA's statistician indicated that the test was significantly correlated with a measure of performance. However, the court rejected the notion of job relatedness because the magnitude of the correlation coefficient was only .107 and was only statistically significant due to the large sample size. In other words, the court ruled that the correlation may have been statistically significant but was not of practical significance.

INTERPRETING CORRELATIONS WITH NOMINAL DATA

Correlations are normally conducted between variables that are measured on ordinal, ratio, and interval scales. That is, variables whose numbers suggest something about their standing relative to other numbers. For example, if we correlate the number of years that employees have been employed by the organization with their current salaries, it would be easy to interpret the correlation coefficient. However, with one exception, correlations cannot be conducted on variables measured with a nominal scale (numbers that represent discreet categories that provide no relative information). For example, suppose that we coded our office locations as (1) Los Angeles, (2) New York, (3) Miami, and (4) Dallas. We then correlate location with salary and obtain a correlation of .40. What would that mean? As location went up, so did salary? Such a correlation would not make sense. Similarly, if we coded employee race as 1=White, 2=African American, 3=Hispanic, and 4=Asian American, what would a correlation mean between salary and race? That as one has more race, his or her salary increases?

The only time we can use a nominal variable in a correlation is when there are only two levels of that variable. An excellent example of this would be employee sex. If we coded men as 0 and women as 1, we can correlate sex with salary and actually have the correlation make sense. That is, with sex coded with men as 0 and women as 1, a positive correlation would mean that average salary for women (the higher code) is greater than the average salary for men (the lower code), and a negative correlation would mean that women are being paid less than men.

PRACTICAL SIGNIFICANCE: IS OUR CORRELATION ANY GOOD?

We have already discussed that the magnitude of a correlation coefficient can range from 0 to 1 and that the farther the coefficient is from zero, the higher the relationship between two variables. But what does a correlation of .40 mean? We know that a correlation of .40 indicates a stronger relationship than a correlation of .20. But, is .40 a high correlation? The answer, of course, is that it depends and there are three common ways to answer this question: variance accounted for, comparison to norms, and utility analysis.

Variance Accounted For (r^2)

One way to add meaning to a correlation coefficient (r) is to square the coefficient. This squared coefficient is most often referred to as r^2 (r squared) but is also called the *coefficient of determination*. As an example, let's imagine that we obtain a correlation of .40 between scores on SAT and grades in college. If we square our coefficient of .40 we would get an r^2 of .16. The .16 indicates that we can explain or predict 16% of the variability in college grades by students' SAT scores. The remaining 84% is explained by such other factors as motivation, interest, luck, and illness.

In general, the r^2 values in psychology and in human resources tend to be relatively low. Why? Because life is complicated and success in school, on a job, or in relationships is due to more than one factor. So, when interpreting the value of r^2, the norms associated with a given field or topic must be considered.

Comparison to Norms

Though we would like to have extremely high correlations and r-squares, as mentioned previously, in psychology and human resources this is rare. So, to interpret a correlation as being "good" or "high," one must compare the magnitude of a correlation with those that are typically obtained in similar situations. As can be seen in Table 4.2, the "typical" correlations found in organizational psychology research vary tremendously by topic.

In personnel selection, correlations between selection tests and measures of performance (validity coefficients) correlations are typically in the .20 to .40 range. Thus, in personnel selection, a correlation below .20 would be considered low, .20 to .29 considered moderate, .30 to .39 high, and .40 or greater as outstanding. Validity coefficients greater than .60 probably indicate one of two things: either the correlation coefficient is suspect (e.g., calculation errors, chance due to small sample size, or cheating) or the personnel analyst deserves the Nobel Prize for science!

If we are using a particular type of selection test and want to compare it to similar tests, Table 4.3 provides an easy way to assess the magnitude of our correlation. For example, if we correlated our assessment center scores with supervisor ratings of performance and obtained a correlation of .15, we can see from Table 4.3 that our validity of .15 is well below the typical validity of .25 for assessment centers. Note to meta-analysis fans—the correlations in the table below are uncorrected. See Aamodt (2007) or Schmidt and Hunter (1998) for tables showing corrected or "true" validities. These concepts will be explained further in Chapter 6 on meta-analysis.

Unfortunately, tables such as 4.2 and 4.3 are not always available that make it easy to compare a correlation coefficient with norms.

Table 4.2

Correlation Norms in Organizational Psychology

Topic	Meta-analysis	Average Correlation
Intrinsic motivation and organizational commitment	Mathieu & Zajac (1990)	.67
Job satisfaction and organizational commitment	Cooper-Hakim & Viswesvaran (2005)	.59
Agreement of performance ratings by two supervisors	Conway & Huffcut (1997)	.50
Absenteeism and lateness	Koslowsky et al. (1997)	.40
Job satisfaction and performance	Judge et al. (2001)	.30
Absenteeism and turnover	Griffth et al. (2000)	.21
Enjoyment of training and actual learning	Alliger et al. (1997)	.11

Table 4.3

Correlation Norms for Employee Selection Validity

Technique	Meta-analysis	Average Validity
Cognitive ability	Schmidt & Hunter (1998)	.39
Biodata	Beall (1991)	.36
Structured interview	Huffcutt & Arthur (1994)	.34
Assessment centers	Arthur et al. (2003)	.28
Work samples	Roth et al. (2005)	.26
Situational judgment	McDaniel et al. (2001)	.26
Experience	Quinones et al. (1995)	.22
Integrity tests	Ones et al. (1993)	.21
References	Aamodt & Williams (2005)	.18
Grades	Roth et al. (1996)	.16
Personality	Tett et al. (1994)	.12
Unstructured interview	Huffcutt & Arthur (1994)	.11

Utility Analysis

Another way to determine if a validity coefficient is "any good" is to translate the correlation into terms that most people can understand. Though there are several different methods used to establish the utility of a test (e.g., Taylor-Russell Tables, expectancy charts), we will concentrate on the Brogden-Cronbach-Gleser Utility Formula. This formula computes the amount of money that an organization would save if it used a test to select employees. To use this formula, six pieces of information must be known.

1. *Number of employees hired per year (n).* This number is easy to determine: it is simply the number of employees who are hired for a given position in a year. This number can be the actual number in a given year or an estimate of the number in a "typical" year.

2. *Average tenure (t).* This is the average number of years that employees in the position tend to stay with the company. The number is computed by using information from company records to identify the time that each employee in that position stayed with the company. The number of years of tenure for each employee is summed and divided by the total number of employees. If actual tenure data are not available, an estimate can be used; but estimates reduce the accuracy of the utility formula.

3. *Test validity (r).* This figure is the criterion validity coefficient that was obtained through a validity study, the technical manual that accompanies a commercially available test, or validity generalization.

4. *Standard deviation of performance in dollars (SD$).* For many years, this number was difficult to compute. Research has shown, however, that for jobs in which performance is normally distributed, a good estimate of

the difference in performance between an average and a good worker (one standard deviation away in performance) is 40% of the employee's annual salary. To obtain this, the total salaries of current employees in the position in question can be averaged, or the salary grade midpoint for the position can be used. For example, if the salary midpoint for an electronics assembler is $25,000, SD$ would be .40 * $25,000 = $10,000.

5.   *Mean standardized predictor score of selected applicants (m).* This number is obtained in one of two ways. The first method is to obtain the average score on the selection test both for the applicants who are hired and the applicants who are not hired. The average test score of the nonhired applicants is subtracted from the average test score of the hired applicants. This difference is divided by the standard deviation of all the test scores.   For example, we administer a test of cognitive ability to a group of 50 applicants and hire the 5 with the highest scores. The average score of the 5 hired applicants is 35.2, the average test score of the other 45 applicants is 28.2, and the standard deviation of all test scores is 8.5. The desired figure would be:

$$(35.2 - 28.2) \div 8.5 = 7.0 \div 8.5 = .647$$

The second way to find *m* is to compute the proportion of applicants who are hired and then use a conversion table to convert the proportion into a standard score. This second method is used when an organization plans to use a test, knows the probable selection ratio based on previous hiring periods, but does not know the average test scores because the organization has never used the test. Using the above example, the proportion of applicants hired would be:

$$\text{openings} \div \text{applicants} = 5 \div 50 = .10$$

From Table 4.4, we see that the standard score associated with a selection ratio of .10 is 1.76.

6. *Cost of testing (C)*. This figure is obtained by multiplying the number of applicants by the cost per test.

To determine the savings to the company, we use the following formula:

$$\text{Savings} = (n)\,(t)\,(r)\,(SD\$)\,(m) \text{ - cost of testing}$$

Table 4.4
Selection ratio conversion table

Selection Ratio	Standard Score (m)
.05	2.08
.10	1.76
.20	1.40
.30	1.17
.40	0.97
.50	0.80
.60	0.64
.70	0.50
.80	0.35
.90	0.20
1.00	0.00

As an example, suppose we will hire 10 auditors per year, the average person in this position stays 2 years, the validity coefficient is .40, and average annual salary for the position is $30,000, and we have 50 applicants for 10 openings. Thus,

$n = 10$
$t = 2$
$r = .40$

$sd\$ = \$30,000 \times .40 = 12,000$
$m = 10/50 = .20 = 1.40$ (.20 is converted to 1.40 by using
the conversion table)
Cost of testing = (50 applicants x $10 = $500)

Using the utility formula, we would have

$$(10)\ (2)\ (.40)\ (12,000)\ (1.40) - (500) = \$133,900$$

This means that after accounting for the cost of testing, using this particular test instead of selecting employees by chance will save a company $133,900 over the two years that auditors typically stay with the organization. Because a company seldom selects employees by chance, the same formula should be used with the validity of the test (interview, psychological test, references, and so on) that the company currently uses. The result of this computation should then be subtracted from the first.

Applying Your Knowledge

You can apply what you have learned in this chapter by reading the following articles in *Applied H.R.M. Research* (www.radford.edu/~applyhrm) and in *Public Personnel Management*.

Cole, M. S., Feild, H. S., & Giles, W. F. (2003). What can we uncover about applicants based on their resumes? A field study. *Applied H.R.M. Research, 8*(2), 51-62.

Gilbert, J. A. (2000). An empirical examination of resources in a diverse environment. *Public Personnel Management, 29*(2), 175-184.

O'Connell, M. S., Doverspike, D., Cober, A. B., & Philips, J. L. (2001). Forging work teams: Effects of the distribution of cognitive ability on team performance. *Applied H.R.M. Research, 6*(2), 115-128.

Smith, W. J., Harrington, K. V., & Houghton, J. D. (2000). Predictors of performance appraisal discomfort: A preliminary examination. *Public Personnel Management, 29*(1), 21-32.

5. Understanding Regression

IN THE LAST CHAPTER, we discussed how correlation is used to show relationships between two variables. Though correlation is the basis for regression, regression analysis allows us to do three things that simple correlations do not: make precise predictions, combine small correlation coefficients, and remove unnecessary variables.

Functions of Regression

MAKING PRECISE PREDICTIONS

Suppose that you conduct a validity study and find that the correlation between scores on a cognitive ability test and performance in the police academy is .45. From these results, you would conclude that the two are highly related and that applicants with high scores on the test will perform better in the academy than applicants with low scores on the test. Though such information is useful, it may not tell us all we need to know. That is, we know that on a *relative* basis, an applicant scoring 85 on the exam should do *better* in the academy than an applicant scoring 75. What we don't know, however, is on an *absolute* basis, how well the applicant will perform in the academy. Will she average 90%? Will she even pass the academy? Regression analysis can help answer such questions by allowing us to take a score on a test, enter it into a regression equation, and obtain an applicant's predicted score on some measure of work performance (e.g., academy grades, supervisor ratings).

71

COMBINING SMALL CORRELATIONS

If you remember from our discussion on correlation, we like to see correlations of at least .20 between a selection test and a measure of job performance. However, suppose that we have a personality inventory that correlates .13 with job performance and a cognitive ability test that correlates .15 with job performance. Based on these small correlations, we would probably be disappointed and lose hope of ever winning the Nobel Prize for HR Validity Studies. However, regression analysis might be able to save the day. That is, with multiple regression, we can combine two small correlations into one larger correlation (if the two predictors do not correlate with one another, we can simply add the squared correlations, but it is usually more complicated than that).

The late industrial psychologist Dan Johnson likened the use of regression to a fishing trip. During our trip, we can try to catch one huge fish to make our meal, or we can catch several small fish that, when cooked and placed on a plate, make the same size meal as one large fish. With selection tests, we try for one or two tests that will correlate with performance at a high level. Unfortunately, such big correlations are as hard to get as it is to catch a fish large enough to feed the entire family. But by combining several tests with smaller validities, we can predict performance as well as we could by using one test with a very high validity.

REMOVING UNNECESSARY VARIABLES

One of the nice things about multiple regression is that in addition to combining small correlations, it also tells us if we have too many variables measuring the same thing. That is, suppose our selection battery contains a personality inventory and an unstructured interview. The personality inventory correlates .25 with performance and the unstructured interview correlates .20 with performance. We start to get excited because if we add the two together, we would have a multiple correlation (R) of .45. However, after entering our data into a regression analysis, we find that our equation "threw out" the interview because it was measuring the same thing our personality test was measuring — social skills and extroversion. So, even though we thought we were measuring two different constructs, our test and interview were actually measuring the same thing (they were highly correlated).

A few years ago, we were asked by a clinical psychologist to validate the test battery he was using to select police officers. As we reviewed his battery, we were stunned to see that every applicant was administered three different measures of cognitive ability and three different personality inventories. When we asked the psychologist why he used so many similar tests, he said that he, "got something different from each one of them." However, since the three cognitive ability measures were highly correlated, as were the three personality inventories (he scores them pass/fail), we doubted that the extra tests provided any new information.

To test this idea, we entered the test scores into two separate regression equations—one to predict his overall ratings of "suitability" and one to predict supervisor ratings of on-the-job performance. As expected, one personality inventory and one cognitive ability test predicted his suitability ratings— the other tests did not help predict his ratings (that is, the other tests did not account for *unique variance*). We were unsuccessful in explaining the results to him in terms of statistics, so we finally said, "What the results show is that you can make the same decisions with two tests as you would with six. The difference is that you will save about $100 in testing costs per applicant." That he understood!

The moral of this story is that when selecting employees, the test battery should not contain several measures of the same knowledge, skill, or ability. If we go back to our example of making a meal, once we catch enough fish (a cognitive ability test), there is no need to catch more (more cognitive ability tests). Instead, to make the perfect meal, we should add a salad (personality inventory), some bread (structured interview), and desert (integrity test). Too much of the same thing makes a boring meal and a wasteful selection battery.

Conducting a Regression Analysis

To conduct a regression analysis, a computer program such as SPSS, SAS, or Excel is typically used. Though each of these programs uses slightly different commands, the results are almost identical. To run a regression analysis, a researcher tells the computer which variables are the predictors (the independent variables) and which variables are the ones to be predicted (the dependent variables). For example,

- A personnel analyst might be interested in seeing how interview scores and scores on five personality dimensions (the predictors) predict supervisor ratings of on-the-job performance (the dependent variable).

- A compensation analyst might want to see how performance ratings, years in the organization, and education level (the predictors) are related to salary (the dependent variable).

- A university might want to find the best way to use SAT scores and high school grade point averages (the predictors) to predict the GPA students will earn during their freshman year (the dependent variable).

TYPES OF REGRESSION ANALYSES

There are two main ways to enter the predictors into the regression analysis: stepwise and hierarchical. With a stepwise regression analysis, the computer takes the best predictor of the dependent variable and enters it into the equation first. The computer then enters the second best predictor and then the third best and so on. The computer stops entering variables when there are either no variables left to enter or the remaining variables do not add a significant amount of prediction. Stepwise regression is the most commonly used method in employee selection.

How does the computer program know which variable is best at each step? The first variable entered into the regression equation is the one with the highest correlation with the dependent variable. The next one entered is determined by two things: how well it is related to the dependent variable and how highly it is correlated with the variable already entered into the equation. As an example, look at the correlations in Table 5.1 that show the relationships between grades in graduate school and GRE scores, undergraduate grades, and reference letters.

In a stepwise regression, GRE scores would be the first predictor entered into the equation, because they have the highest correlation with the dependent variable (graduate GPA). Although undergraduate grades have the next highest correlation ($r = .25$), references ($r = .20$) would actually be the next entered; because, although undergraduate GPA has a higher correlation than do references, they are so highly correlated ($r = .80$) with GRE scores that they would not add much unique or incremental prediction. References, however, are not at all correlated with GRE scores ($r = .00$) and thus will add incremental prediction.

Table 5.1
Correlations with Graduate GPA

	Grad GPA	GRE	UG GPA	References
Graduate GPA	1.00	.30	.25	.20
GRE		1.00	.80	.00
Undergraduate GPA			1.00	.10
References				1.00

With a hierarchical regression analysis, the researcher tells the computer program the order in which to enter the predictors. There are many times when a researcher might want to dictate the order. For example, a police department has developed a structured interview and intends to use it as the main method of selecting new officers. The department is considering adding a cognitive ability test to its selection battery and wants to know if the cognitive ability test will increase the prediction accuracy above that already provided by the interview. In such a case, the department would first enter interview scores into the regression analysis and then the cognitive ability scores. If the cognitive ability scores are statistically significant (i.e., provide *incremental validity*), the department would use both the interview and the cognitive ability test. If the addition of the cognitive ability test is not significant, the department would use only the structured interview.

Another reason to use hierarchical regression is to reduce adverse impact. For example, suppose that a police department plans to use a structured interview and a cognitive ability test to select new officers. The cognitive ability test correlates .30 with performance, and the structured interview correlates .20 with performance. The cognitive interview is moderately correlated with the structured interview. When used together in a stepwise regression, the interview and the test correlate .35 with police performance.

Though the department is happy with the validity of the two tests, it is concerned because their selection battery has adverse impact against African Americans. After analyzing the data further, the department finds that the adverse impact is due to the cognitive ability test—African Americans and Whites score equally well on the structured interview.

Because of the adverse impact, the department considers dropping the cognitive ability test but doesn't want to do that because the test is valid. In this case, hierarchical regression might be a partial solution. By entering the structured interview into the equation first, it will carry more weight than it would in a stepwise regression equation. By increasing the weight given to the predictor with no adverse impact, the adverse impact of the entire selection procedure will be reduced (but not eliminated).

Hierarchical regression is also commonly used in salary equity analysis. For example, suppose that a school system discovers that the average salary for its 30 female janitors is $17,232 compared to $20,400 for its 50 male janitors. The Department of Labor thinks this difference is due to discrimination. The school system, however, thinks that the difference in average salary is due to the number of years the employees have been with the school system and to their performance ratings rather than to sex discrimination.

To test its idea, the school system would first enter the employees' tenure and performance rating data into the analysis and then enter the employees' gender (coded as 0 for males, 1 for females). If gender did not enter the equation as a significant predictor of salary, it could be said that the salary differences were indeed due to tenure and performance. If gender entered the equation as a significant predictor, two interpretations could be made. The first is that the school system is discriminating. The second is that there are other unknown variables (e.g., education level) that could explain the salary difference if they were entered into the regression equation.

CONSIDERATIONS IN RUNNING A REGRESSION ANALYSIS

For a regression analysis to be accurate, three factors should be considered: number of subjects, variables in the regression model, and missing data.

Number of Subjects

Though computer programs will allow you to run a regression analysis with data from two or more subjects, the results are not as accurate (stable) when a small number of subjects (e.g., applicants, employees) is used. The question of how many subjects are needed to reliably run a regression analysis is a difficult one to answer and depends in part on the purpose of the regression analysis. If the purpose of the regression analysis is to *explain* what is happening in a series of data (e.g., Are men and women at a particular company being paid equitably? What factors are associated with absenteeism on the night shift?), fewer subjects are needed than if the purpose is to *predict* the behavior of people not in the sample (e.g., using employee data from 1999-2005 to predict how future employees will behave).

So, how many subjects do you need? The answer depends on who you ask. Some statisticians argue that there is a minimum number of subjects that must be present to conduct a regression analysis (e.g., 50), some argue that the key is ratio of subjects to the number of variables (e.g., 10 subjects for every predictor), and others argue that both a minimum number and the subjects-to-variable ratio are important (e.g., a minimum of 30 subjects *and* at least 10 subjects per predictor).

In general, regression used to explain data can be comfortably used when you have data from 50 or more people. Regressions can be run with data from fewer people, but caution should be used when interpreting the results.

Variables in the Regression Model

Model Specification. One of the assumptions in regression is that all relevant variables are included in the model and no irrelevant variables are included. For example, suppose that you were trying to predict graduate GPA and theorized that grades in graduate school are the result of both cognitive ability and motivation. If your regression equation only included GRE scores (a measure of cognitive ability) but no measure of motivation (e.g., undergraduate GPA, letters of recommendation, personal statement), you would have a *model specification* error. Thus it is important to try to first theorize or brainstorm the relevant variables and then make a strong effort to include them in your regression.

Singularity and Multicollinearity. There are times when two variables in a regression equation are either perfectly correlated (singularity) or so highly correlated (multicollinearity) with each other that problems in the regression equation occur. An example of singularity would be if you were trying to predict employee salary and your variables included years with the company and total years of experience. Normally, these values for most employees would be different. That is, an employee might have 5 years with the company and 10 years of total experience (5 with the company and 5 with other companies). In the case of an entry level job, however, it might be that the number of years with the company is the same as the total years of experience. In such a case, one of the two variables would need to be removed for the regression equation to run.

With a case of singularity, the regression equation will not even run. With multicollinearity, however, the equation will run, but the regression weights will not be accurate. These inaccurate regression weights might result in an important variable appearing to be unrelated to the dependent variable or appearing to be related in a negative direction even though the actual relationship is positive.

Though there is some disagreement among statisticians, two variables need to be correlated at least .90, and probably higher, for multicollinearity to be a concern. If two variables do correlate that highly, the easiest solution is to simply remove one of the variables from the regression analysis.

Missing Data

Suppose you have 100 employees in your organization and want to see how well the employees' cognitive ability, education level, and interview scores predict their supervisors' ratings of their performance. Of the 100 employees, you have interview scores for all of them, education levels for 95 employees, and cognitive ability scores for 70 employees. If you ran a regression, only the 70 employees with all three scores could be included in the analysis.

There are three common ways to handle missing data.

The easiest is to *remove the employees* with missing data and run the regression only with the employees who have no missing data. Another approach is to *remove the variables* that have missing data and run the regression using only those variables for which data are not missing. The third approach is to *substitute the mean* value of the variable for the missing data. That is if the mean in the company is 5 years of prior experience, and experience data are missing for Joe and Sue, we would give both Joe and Sue a value of 5 years.

The choice of the three methods to use is largely dependent on the percentage of data that are missing. For example, if you have data from 100 employees and data are missing on a variable for 2 of the 100 employees, the best solution would probably be to remove the employees with the missing data. If, however, data on a variable are missing from half of the employees, it would make more sense to remove the variable from the analysis.

Interpreting Regression Results

Most statistical programs such as SAS and SPSS produce output with similar information and tables. The output can best be interpreted by breaking it into three sets of information: effectiveness of the regression analysis, analysis of variance results, and information about the independent variables.

To explain how to interpret these three sets of information, we will use two examples. One of the examples comes from a company that wanted to determine the extent to which three factors (years with the company, having a bachelor's degree, and performance ratings) explained how much its employees were being paid. The other example is a regression analysis used at Radford University to select I/O psychology graduate students using the students' undergraduate GPAs, scores on the Graduate Record Exam (GRE), and reference ratings provided by faculty members.

Table 5.2
Regression statistics

| | Example | |
	Salary Study	Graduate School Admissions
Observations	33	232
Multiple R	0.53	0.47
R-square	0.28	0.22
Adjusted R^2	0.21	0.21
Standard error	$2,160	0.39

EFFECTIVENESS OF THE REGRESSION ANALYSIS

The first set of information that is reported in most journal articles or technical reports summarizes the overall effectiveness of the regression analysis. As shown in Table 5.2, five pieces of information are usually provided: number of observations, multiple R, R-squared, adjusted R^2, and the standard error of the estimate.

Observations

Observations are the number of employees included in the analysis. As mentioned previously, the greater the number of observations, the more accurate and stable the results of the regression. In the salary study, our regression analysis is based on data from only 33 employees; whereas, in our graduate admissions study, our regression analysis is based on data from 232 students.

Multiple R

The *Multiple R* is the correlation between the *combination* of the independent variables and the dependent variable. From Table 5.2, you can see that for the salary study, the combination of time-in-company, bachelor's degree, and performance ratings correlates .53 with employee salaries. For the graduate admissions study, the combination of undergraduate GPA, GRE scores, and reference ratings correlates .47 with the GPA students obtained in graduate school.

R-Square (R²)

R-Square (R²) is the percentage of individual differences in the dependent variable that the regression model explains. As shown in Table 5.2, the combination of time-in-company, bachelor's degree, and performance ratings accounts for 28% of the individual differences in employee pay (.53 * .53). We are not sure what accounts for the additional 72%. For the graduate admissions study, the combination of undergraduate GPA, GRE scores, and reference ratings accounts for 22% of the variability in graduate school grades (.47*.47).

Adjusted R²

Regression is most accurate with large sample sizes. The *Adjusted R-square* corrects for estimated errors caused by small sample sizes. The larger the sample size, the smaller the difference between the R² and the adjusted R². In Table 5.2, the R² of .28 for the salary study was adjusted downward to .21 and the R² of .22 for the graduate admissions study was adjusted downward to .21. Notice that because the graduate admissions study has a much larger sample size (232) than does the salary study (33), the adjusted R² did not decline as much.

Standard Error of the Estimate

As mentioned earlier in the chapter, regression can be used to make predictions. In the salary study, the goal was to "predict" or "estimate" what an employee's salary should be given his/her years in the company, education, and performance. Because estimates made from a regression equation are just that—estimates—most regression output includes the *Standard Error of the Estimate*. The greater the R² and the sample size, the smaller the standard error of the estimate.

As shown in Table 5.2, for the salary study, the standard error of $2,160 indicates that 68% (one standard deviation from the mean) of the errors in estimating what an employee's salary should be will fall within $2,160. Stated another way, if we estimate that an employee should be paid $45,000, we are 68% confident that their salary should be between $42,840 ($45,000 - $2,160) and $47,160 ($45,000 + $2,160). So, if we estimate that an employee should make $45,000 and she is actually making $44,000, we would probably not be concerned that the employee is underpaid; because her actual salary ($44,000) falls within one standard error ($42,840 - $47,160) of the estimated salary. Though our example used one standard error, most HR professionals use a criterion of two standard errors.

For the graduate admissions study, the standard error of the estimate was .39, indicating that if we predict that a student will earn a graduate GPA of 3.6, we would expect that 68% of the time their actual graduate GPA will be between 3.21 (3.60 - .39) and 3.99 (3.60 + .39).

ANALYSIS OF VARIANCE RESULTS

The next section of the output depicts the results of the analysis of variance (ANOVA) that tests the statistical significance of the R^2. The key part of this section is the significance level ($p <$ column). If the significance level is less than or equal to .05, the R^2 discussed in the previous section is considered statistically significant. In the output shown in Table 5.3, the significance level of .02 would indicate that the R^2 of .28 from the salary study is statistically significant.

Table 5.3
ANOVA table for the salary study regression analysis

Source	df	Sum of Squares	Mean Square	F	$p <$
Regression	3	53,164,088.63	17,721,362,88	3.80	0.02
Residual	29	135,373,606.01	4,668,055.38		
Total	32	188.537.694.64			

Table 5.4
ANOVA table for the graduate admissions regression

Source	df	Sum of Squares	Mean Square	F	p <
Regression	3	9.97	3.32	21.96	0.000
Residual	228	34.50	0.15		
Total	231	44.47			

For the graduate admissions study ANOVA in Table 5.4, notice that the probability value is 0.000. This also indicates that the R^2 is statistically significant. Most programs round probability levels to two or three decimal places. As a result, if you see a probability value of .00 or .000, it means that the probability that the results occurred by chance is lower than 1 in a hundred for the .00 figure and 1 in a thousand for the .000 figure, both of which are statistically significant.

Although the other numbers in the tables are only important because they provide the data necessary to get the significance level, in case you are interested, here is what the other columns mean.

Degrees of Freedom

The "df" column indicates the degrees of freedom. The regression degrees of freedom are the number of independent variables in the analysis. In both examples, we have three independent variables: years with the company, education, and performance ratings for the salary study and undergraduate GPA, GRE scores, and reference ratings for the graduate admissions study. Thus, for both studies, we have three regression degrees of freedom. The total degrees of freedom are the number of observations minus one. In the salary study, because we have 33 observations, we have 32 total degrees of freedom. In the graduate admissions study, because we have 232 observations, we have 231 total degrees of freedom. The residual degrees of freedom are simply the total degrees of freedom minus the regression degrees of freedom.

Sum of Squares, Mean Square, and F

The sums of squares and the mean square are used to compute

the F value that you learned about in Chapter 3. The mean square is computed by dividing the sum of squares by the degrees of freedom and the F value is computed by dividing the regression mean square by the residual (or error) mean square.

INFORMATION ABOUT THE INDEPENDENT VARIABLES

The final section of the output contains information about each of the independent variables included in the regression analysis. The first key value for each variable is the p-value, which is the significance level. If this value is less than or equal to .05, the variable explains a statistically significant percentage of the individual differences in your dependent variable. In the salary study example shown in Table 5.5, time in company (tenure) with a p-value of .00 is statistically significant but having a bachelor's degree ($p < .13$) and performance ratings are not ($p < .89$).

When looking at the significance levels for the independent variables, three patterns can emerge: all variables will be statistically significant, none of the variables will be statistically significant, or some, but not all, of the variables will be statistically significant. If none of the variables are significant, you can't use the regression model to understand current behavior or to predict/estimate future/desired behavior.

In the graduate admissions study shown in Table 5.6, both GPA ($p < .000$) and GRE scores ($p < .000$) are statistically significant but reference ratings ($p < .118$) are not.

Table 5.5
Information about the independent variables in the salary study

Variable	Coefficient	Standard Error	t-value	p-value	Beta
Intercept	$19,756.00	$668.97	29.53	0.00	0.00
Tenure	$318.82	$103.69	3.07	0.00	0.74
Degree	- $983.32	$625.57	-1.57	0.13	-0.39
Performance	- $96.58	$693.77	-0.14	0.89	-0.02

Table 5.6
Information about the independent variables in the graduate admissions study

Variable	Coefficient	Standard Error	t-value	p-value	Beta
Intercept	1.13	.321	3.52	.001	
GPA	.383	.076	5.03	.000	.337
GRE	.001	.000	3.59	.000	.211
References	.136	.087	1.57	.118	.105

The second part of the output that provides useful information is the coefficient column. For each variable, the coefficient indicates the amount of change in the dependent variable for each unit of change in the dependent variable. For example, in Table 5.5, the coefficient of $318.82 for tenure indicates that for every year the employee has been with the company, his or her salary would be expected to be $318.82 above the intercept coefficient of $19,756. So, if Marcus has been with the company for 10 years, we would estimate that his salary should be $22,944.20 [$19,756 + (10*$318.82)] and if Mary has been with the company for 5 years we would estimate that her salary should be $21,350.10 [$19,756 + 5*$318.82)].

For the graduate admissions example, the coefficient of .383 indicates that for every full point of undergraduate GPA, we would expect an increase in graduate GPA of .383. That is, the expected difference in graduate GPAs between an applicant with an undergraduate GPA of 3.00 and one with an undergraduate GPA of 4.00 would be .383.

Notice in Tables 5.5 and 5.6 that there is a column with the heading, "Beta." Though Beta is not commonly used to interpret regression results, it is the standardized regression coefficient. The further that the Beta value is from zero, the stronger the relationship between the independent variable and the dependent variable.

THE REGRESSION EQUATION

From our salary study and graduate admissions examples above, we know we can predict employee salaries and graduate GPAs. To use our regression results to make specific predictions, we need to create a regression equation. In its simplest form, the results of a regression analysis yield a regression equation that looks something like:

$$Y = c + (b1)(x1)$$

Where Y is the predicted value of some variable, c is a constant (in algebra, we would call this the intercept which represents the predicted score on the criterion if the scores on the predictor were zero), b1 is the weight we give our predictor (in algebra we would call this the slope which represents the amount of change we would expect in the predictor for each unit of change in the predictor), and x1 is the score on a predictor. Though the constant and the weight can be calculated by hand, we normally let the computer do the work by using a program such as SAS, SPSS, or Excel.

To use our regression results from Table 5.6, our regression equation to predict graduate school grades would be:

Predicted grad GPA = 1.13 + (.383) (UG GPA) + (.001) (GRE) + (.136) (reference score)

In the equation:
- .13 is the constant (intercept)
- .383 is the weight that is multiplied by the undergraduate GPA
- .001 is the weight that is multiplied by the GRE score
- .136 is the weight that is multiplied by the reference rating (the reference rating is on a 1-4 scale with a 4 being excellent and a 1 being below average).

Let's use two hypothetical students as an example. Jenny Craig has a GRE score of 1000, an undergraduate GPA of 3.60, and a reference rating score of 3.0. Richard Simmons has a GRE score of 900, an undergraduate GPA of 3.0 and a reference rating score of 3.5. The formula to predict the students' graduate GPAs would be:

Jenny's GPA
$$= 1.13 + (.383)\,(3.60) + (.001)\,(1000) + (.136)\,(3.0)$$
$$= 1.13 + 1.38 + 1.00 + 0.41$$
$$= 3.92$$

Richard's GPA
$$= 1.13 + (.383)\,(3.00) + (.001)\,(900) + (.136)\,(2.0)$$
$$= 1.13 + 1.15 + 0.90 + .272$$
$$= 3.45$$

At Radford University, we typically have about 80 students apply for our 12 openings so we only accept students whose predicted graduate GPA is at least a 3.60. Using the data from the above example, we would accept Jenny and her 3.92 predicted GPA and reject Richard and his 3.45 predicted GPA.

Final Thought

When running a regression or reading about a regression analysis in a journal or technical report, you can use the questions in Box 5.1 to evaluate the analysis. If the answer to any of the questions is "no," there may be a problem with the analysis.

Box 5.1
Checklist for evaluating journal articles and technical reports using regression

?	Assessment Question
	Are there at least 30 total subjects and at least 5 subjects per variable?
	Are all relevant variables included in the regression?
	Is the model free of irrelevant variables?
	Is the hypothesized relationship between the independent and dependent variables linear?
	If the hypothesized relationship is not linear, did the researcher test for curvilinear relationships (e.g., standardize and then square the variable)?
	Did the researcher search for and remove outliers?
	Are the correlations among the independent variables less than .90?

Applying Your Knowledge

You can apply what you have learned in this chapter by reading the following articles in *Applied H.R.M. Research* (www.radford.edu/~applyhrm) and in *Public Personnel Management.*

Befort, N. & Hattrup, K. (2003). Valuing task and contextual performance: Experience, job roles, and ratings of the importance of job behaviors. *Applied H.R.M. Research, 8*(1), 17-32.

Huang, I, Chuang, C. J., & Lin, H. (2003). The role of burnout in the relationship between perceptions of organizational politics and turnover intentions. *Public Personnel Management, 32*(4), 519-530.

Raynes, B. L. (2001). Predicting difficult employees: The relationship between vocational interests, self-esteem, and problem communication styles. *Applied H.R.M. Research, 6*(1), 33-66.

Roberts, G. E. (2003). Municipal government part-time employee benefits practices. *Public Personnel Management, 32*(3), 435-454.

6. Meta-Analysis

IN THE OLD DAYS (prior to 1980), research was reviewed by reading all of the articles on a topic and then drawing a conclusion. For example, suppose that a personnel analyst was asked to review the literature to see if education was related to police performance. The analyst would find every article on the topic, perhaps count the articles that showed significant results, and then reach a conclusion such as, "Given that eight articles showed significant results and nine did not, we must conclude that education is not related to police performance."

Problems with Traditional Literature Reviews

Unfortunately, there are three common situations in which such a conclusion might be inaccurate: small but consistent relationships, moderate relationships but small sample sizes, and large differences in sample sizes across studies.

SMALL BUT CONSISTENT CORRELATIONS

Suppose that you find four studies investigating the relationship between education and police performance, but none of the four studies reported a significant relationship between the two variables. With a traditional review, you would probably conclude that education is not a significant predictor of police performance. However, it might be that the actual relationship between education and performance is relatively small, and a large number of subjects would have been needed in each study to detect this small relationship.

Take for example the studies shown in Table 6.1. You have four studies, each with samples of 50 officers. The correlations between education level and performance in the four studies are .20, .17, .19, and .16. Though the size of the coefficients is consistent across the four studies, none of the correlations by itself is statistically significant due to the combination of small correlations and small sample sizes in each study. If all four studies are combined in a meta-analysis however, we find that the average correlation is .18 and with a sample size of 200, the correlation would be statistically significant.

MODERATE RELATIONSHIPS AND SMALL SAMPLE SIZES

A second situation in which traditional literature reviews often draw incorrect conclusions occurs when the correlations in the previous studies are moderate or high, but the sample sizes were too low for the relationship to be statistically significant. Take for example the four studies shown in Table 6.2. Each of the correlations is at what we would consider a high level, yet the correlations would not be statistically significant due to the small sample sizes in each study. If we combined the four studies however, we would get an average correlation of .41—with a total sample size of 80, this would be statistically significant.

LARGE DIFFERENCES IN SAMPLE SIZES ACROSS STUDIES

Another reason that we might incorrectly conclude that education does not predict performance is that differences in correlations across studies may be due to large differences in sample sizes across studies. As you can see in the example shown in Table 6.3, the reason our traditional review would find mixed results is that the two studies showing a low correlation between education and performance had very small sample sizes. Thus, what seem to be huge differences in validity are actually differences due to *sampling error* caused by small sample sizes.

Table 6.1
Example of a Small But Consistent Relationship

Study	Correlation	Sample Size
Aaron (1991)	.22	50
Ruth (1992)	.19	50
Mays (1993)	.21	50
McGuire (1994)	.18	50

Table 6.2
Example of Large Correlations but Small Sample Sizes

Study	Correlation	Sample Size
Spencer (1998)	.43	20
Magnum (1997)	.38	20
Rockford (1992)	.45	20
Mannix (1988)	.39	20

Table 6.3
Example of Inconsistent Sample Sizes

Study	Correlation	Sample Size
Sullivan (1998)	.35	400
Davis (1997)	.05	20
Boscorelli (1992)	.40	290
Yokus (1988)	.10	20

To better understand sampling error, imagine that you have a bowl containing three red balls, three white balls, and three blue balls. You are asked to close your eyes and pick three balls from the bowl. Because there are equal numbers of red, white, and blue balls in the bowl, you would expect to draw one of each color. However, in any given draw from the bowl, it is unlikely that you will get one of each color. If you have no life and draw three balls at a time for ten hours, you might get three red balls on some draws, no white balls on other draws, and three white balls on other draws. Thus, even though we know there are an equal number of each color of ball, any one draw may or may not represent what we know is "the truth." However, over the 10 hours you are drawing balls, the most common draw will be one of each color — a finding consistent with what we know is in the bag.

The same is true in research. Suppose we know that the true correlation between education level and performance is .20. A study at one agency might yield a correlation of .10, another agency might report a correlation of .50, and yet another agency might report a correlation of .30. If all three studies had small samples, the differences among the studies and differences from the "truth" might be due purely to sampling error. This is where meta-analysis saves the day.

Meta-analysis is a statistical method for combining research results. Since the first meta-analysis was published by Gene Glass in 1976, the number of published meta-analyses has increased tremendously;and the methodology has become increasingly complex. The meta-analysis pioneers were Frank Schmidt and John Hunter, and almost every meta-analysis uses the methods they suggested in their 1990 book *Methods of Meta-Analysis* and clarified in the book *Conducting Meta-Analysis using SAS* by Winfred Arthur, Winston Bennett, and Allen Huffcutt.

Though meta-analyses will vary somewhat in their methods and their purpose, most meta-analyses involving personnel selection issues try to answer three questions:

1. What is the mean validity coefficient found in the literature for a given predictor (e.g., interviews, assessment centers, cognitive ability)?

2. If we had a perfect measure of the predictor (e.g., intelligence, computer knowledge), a perfect measure of performance, and no restriction in range, what would be the "true correlation" between our construct and performance?

3. Can we generalize the meta-analysis results to every agency (validity generalization), or is our construct a better predictor of performance in some situations than in others (e.g., large vs. small departments, police departments vs. sheriff's offices)?

Conducting a Meta-Analysis

FINDING STUDIES

The first step in a meta-analysis is to locate studies on the topic of interest. It is common to use both an "active search" and a "passive search." An active search tries to identify every research study within a given parameter. For example, a meta-analyst might concentrate her active search on journal articles and dissertations published between 1970 and 2001 and referenced in one of three computerized literature data bases (PsycInfo, InfoTrac, Dissertation Abstracts International) or referenced in an article found during the computer search. A passive search might include queries to professionals known to be experts in the area, papers presented at conferences, or technical reports known to the author.

The major difference between an active and passive search is that the goal of an active search is to include *every* relevant study within the given parameters, whereas the goal of the passive search is to find other relevant research without any thought that every study on the topic was found. Though this may not seem much of a difference, it is. These days, there are so many potential sources for research—thousands of journals, conference presentations, theses, dissertations, technical reports, and unpublished research articles—that relevant studies are going to be missed. Thus,the credibility of a meta-analysis hinges on the scope and inclusion accuracy of its active search.

CHOOSING STUDIES TO INCLUDE IN THE META-ANALYSIS

Once all of the relevant studies on a topic have been located, the next step is to determine which of these studies will be included in the meta-analysis. To be included in a meta-analysis, an article must report the results of an empirical investigation and include a correlation coefficient, another statistic (e.g., F, t, chi-square) that could be converted to a correlation coefficient, or tabular data that can be entered into the computer to yield a correlation coefficient (many meta-analyses use Cohen's D rather than a correlation coefficient but the rules to include an article are the same). Articles that report results without the above statistics (e.g., "we found a significant relationship between education and academy performance" or "we didn't see any real differences between our educated and uneducated officers") cannot be included in a meta-analysis.

Often, meta-analysts will have other rules about keeping studies. For example, in a meta-analysis on employee-wellness programs, the researcher's decision to include only studies using both pre- and post-measures of absenteeism as well as experimental and control groups resulted in only three usable studies.

CONVERTING RESEARCH FINDINGS TO CORRELATIONS

Once research articles have been located and the decision is made as to which articles to include, statistical results (e.g., F, t, Chi-square) that need to be converted into correlation coefficients are done using the formulas provided in Rosenthal (1985). In some cases, raw data or data listed in tables can be entered into a statistical program (e.g. SAS, SPSS) to directly determine a correlation coefficient.

CUMULATING VALIDITY COEFFICIENTS

As shown in Table 6.4, after the individual correlation

coefficients have been computed, the validity coefficient for each study is weighted by the size of the sample and summed. This procedure ensures that larger studies— presumed to be more accurate—carry more weight than smaller studies. For example, in Table 6.4, the .23 correlation reported by Briscoe is multiplied by the sample size of 150 to get 34.5. This procedure is then done for each of the studies. In addition to the mean validity coefficient, the observed variance, amount of variance expected due to sampling error, and a 95% confidence interval are calculated (it is beyond the scope of this chapter to discuss these calculations).

CORRECTING FOR ARTIFACTS

When conducting a meta-analysis, it is desirable to adjust correlation coefficients to correct for error associated with predictor unreliability, criterion unreliability, restriction of range, and a host of other artifacts (see Hunter & Schmidt, 1990 for a thorough discussion). These adjustments answer the second question of, "If we had perfect measures of the construct, a perfect measure of performance, and no restriction in range, what would be the 'true correlation' between our construct and performance?"

Table 6.4
Example of Cumulating Validity Coefficients

Study	Correlation	Sample Size	Correlation x Sample Size
Briscoe (1997)	.23	150	34.5
Green (1974)	.10	100	10.0
Curtis (1982)	.42	50	21.0
Logan (1991)	.27	300	81.0
Ceretta (1995)	.01	20	0.2
Greevy (1989)	.29	200	58.0
TOTAL		820	204.8

Weighted Average = 204.8 ÷ 820 = .25

Table 6.5
Correcting Correlations for Test Unreliability

Study	Validity	Test Reliability	Square-Root	Corrected Validity
Tinkers (1985)	.30	.92	.96	.31
Evers (1990)	.23	.80	.89	.26
Chance (1995)	.25	.65	.81	.31

These adjustments can be made in one of two ways. The most desirable way is to correct the validity coefficient from each study based on the predictor reliability, criterion reliability, and restriction of range associated with that particular study. A simple example of this process is shown in Table 6.5. To correct the validity coefficients in each study for test unreliability, the validity coefficient is divided by the square root of the reliability coefficient. In the Tinkers (1985) study, the reliability of the test was .92, the square root of .92 is .96, and the corrected validity coefficient is $.30 \div .96 = .31$.

When the necessary information is not available for each study, the mean validity coefficient is corrected rather than each individual coefficient. This is the most common practice. The numbers used to make these corrections come either from the average of information found in the studies that provided reliability or range restriction information or from other meta-analyses. For example, an estimate of the reliability of supervisor ratings of overall performance (r=.52) can be borrowed from the meta-analysis on rating reliability by Viswesvaran, Ones, and Schmidt (1996).

SEARCHING FOR MODERATORS

Being able to generalize meta-analysis findings across all similar organizations and settings (validity generalization) is an important goal of any meta-analysis. It is standard practice in meta-analysis to generalize results when at least 75% of the observed variability in validity coefficients can be attributed to sampling error. When less than 75% can be attributed to sampling error, a search is conducted to find variables that might moderate the size of the validity coefficient. For example, education might predict performance better in larger police departments than in smaller ones.

The idea behind this 75% rule is that due to sampling error, we expect correlations to differ from study to study. The question is, are the differences we observe just sampling error, or do they represent real differences in studies? That is, is the difference between the correlation of .30 found in one study and the correlation of .20 found in another study due to sampling error; or is the difference due to one study being conducted in an urban police department and the other being conducted in a rural department?

To answer this question there are formulas that tell us how much variability in studies we have in our meta-analysis and how much of that variability would be expected due to sampling error.

Understanding Meta-Analysis Results

Now that you have an idea about how a meta-analysis is conducted, let's talk about how to understand meta-analysis results that you might find in a published article. In Table 6.6, you will find the partial results of a meta-analysis we conducted on the relationship between cognitive ability and police performance. The numbers in the table represent the validity of cognitive ability in predicting academy grades and supervisor ratings of performance as a police officer.

Table 6.6 Sample meta-analysis results for cognitive ability

Criterion	K	N	r	95% Confidence Interval		ρ	90% Credibility Interval		SE%	Q_w
				Lower	Upper		Lower	Upper		
Academy grades	61	14,437	.41	.33	.48	.62	.44	.81	78%	77.82
Supervisor ratings	61	16,231	.16	.12	.20	.27	.14	.40	80%	76.40

K=number of studies, N=sample size, r = mean correlation, ρ = mean correlation corrected for range restriction, criterion unreliability, and predictor reliability, SE% = percentage of variance explained by sampling error and study artifacts

NUMBER OF STUDIES AND SAMPLE SIZE

The "K" column indicates the number of studies included in the meta-analysis, and the "N" column indicates the number of total subjects in the studies. There is not a "magical number" of studies that we look for, but a meta-analysis with 20 studies is clearly more useful than one with five.

MEAN OBSERVED VALIDITY COEFFICIENT

The "r" column represents the mean validity coefficient across all studies (weighted by the size of the sample). This coefficient answers our question about the typical validity coefficient found in validation studies on the topic of cognitive ability and police performance. On the basis of our meta-analysis, we would conclude that the validity of cognitive ability in predicting academy grades is .41, and the validity of cognitive ability in predicting supervisor ratings on-the-job performance is .16.

CONFIDENCE INTERVAL

To determine if our observed validity coefficient is "statistically significant," we look at the next two columns which represent the lower and upper limits to our 95% confidence interval. If the interval includes zero, we cannot say that our mean validity coefficient is significant. From the figures in Table 6.6, we would conclude that cognitive ability is a significant predictor of grades in the academy (our confidence interval is .33 - .48) and performance as a police officer (our confidence interval is .12 - .20). Using confidence intervals we can communicate our findings with a sentence such as "Though our best estimate of the validity of cognitive ability in predicting academy performance is .41, we are 95% confident that the validity is no lower than .33 and no higher than .48." It is important to note that some meta-analyses use 80%, 85%, or

90% confidence intervals. The choice of confidence interval levels is a reflection of how conservative a meta-analyst wants to be: the more cautious one wants to be in interpreting the meta-analysis results, the higher the confidence interval used.

CORRECTIONS FOR ARTIFACTS

The column labeled ρ (rho) represents our mean validity coefficient corrected for criterion unreliability, predictor unreliability, and range restriction. This coefficient represents what the "true validity" of cognitive ability would be if we had a perfectly reliable measure of cognitive ability, a perfectly reliable measure of academy grades and supervisor ratings of performance, and no range restriction. Notice how our observed correlations of .41 and .16 increased to .62 and .27 after being corrected for artifacts. When encountering ρ, it is important to consider how many of the artifacts were corrected for. That is, two meta-analyses on the same topic might yield different results if one meta-analysis corrected for all three artifacts while another only corrected for criterion unreliability.

CREDIBILITY INTERVAL

Credibility intervals are used to determine if the corrected correlation coefficient (ρ) is statistically significant and if there are moderators present. Whereas a standard deviation is used to compute a confidence interval, the standard error is used to compute a credibility interval. As with confidence intervals, if a credibility interval includes zero, the corrected correlation coefficient is not statistically significant. If a credibility interval contains zero or is large, the conclusion to be drawn is that the corrected validity coefficient cannot be generalized and that moderators are operating (Arthur, Bennett, & Huffcutt, 2001). When reading a meta-analysis table, be careful because the abbreviation CI is often used both for confidence and credibility intervals.

PERCENTAGE OF VARIANCE DUE TO SAMPLING ERROR

The next column in a meta-analysis table represents the percentage of observed variance that is due to sampling error and study artifacts (SE%). Notice that for grades and performance, these percentages are 78% and 80% respectively. Because the percentage is greater than 75, we can generalize our findings and not have to search for moderators. Such a finding is desired, but is unusual. More typical is the meta-analysis results shown in Table 6.7. These results are from the excellent meta-analysis of the relationship between grades in school and work performance that was conducted by Roth, BeVier, Switzer, and Shippmann (1996).

Roth and his colleagues found that only 54% of the observed variance in correlations would have been expected by sampling error and study artifacts. Because of this, they were forced to search for moderators. They hypothesized that the level of education where the grades were earned (undergraduate, masters, or doctoral program) might moderate the validity of how well grades predicted work performance. As you can see from the table, the validity of grades in master's degree programs was higher than in doctoral programs and that sampling error and study artifacts explained 100% of the variability across studies for these two levels. However, sampling error and study artifacts accounted for only 66% of the observed variance in correlations for grades earned at the bachelor's level. So, the researchers further broke the bachelor's level grades down by the years since graduation.

Rather than using the 75% rule, some meta-analyses will report a Q_w or H_w statistic. If this statistic is significant, then a search for moderators must be made. If the statistic is not significant, we can generalize our findings. As shown back in Table 6.6, the Q_w statistic was not significant for either academy grades or supervisor ratings of performance. This lack of significance is consistent with the fact that sampling error and study artifacts accounted for at least 75% of the observed variance.

Table 6.7

Meta-Analysis of Grades and Work Performance

Criterion	K	N	r	r_{cr}	$r_{cr.rr}$	$r_{cr.rr.pr}$	80% C.I.	SE%
Overall	71	13,984	.16	.23	.32	.35	.30 - .41	54
Education Level								
B.A.	49	9,458	.16	.23	.33	.36	.30 - .42	66
M.A.	4	446	.23	.33	.46	.50	.31 - .56	100
Ph.D./M.D.	6	1,755	.07	.10	.14	.15	.08 - .25	100
Years since graduation								
1 year	13	1,288	.23	.32	.45	.49	.40 - .62	89
2-5 years	11	1,562	.15	.21	.30	.33	.23 - .48	80
6+ years	4	866	.05	.08	.11	.12	.00 - .41	59

A good example of the use of this statistic can be found in a meta-analysis of the effect of flextime and compressed workweeks on work-related behavior (Baltes, Briggs, Huff, Wright, & Neuman, 1999). As you can see in Table 6.8, the asterisks in the final column indicate a significant Q_w, forcing a search for moderators. Note that this meta-analysis used the d statistic rather than an r (correlation) as the effect size. In this example, a d of .30 is equivalent to an r of .15.

Table 6.8

Meta-Analysis of Flextime and Compressed Work Weeks

Variable	K	N	D	95% CI		Q_w
				Lower	Upper	
Flextime	41	4,492	.30	.26	.35	1004.55**
Compressed work week	25	2,921	.29	.23	.34	210.58**

Applying Your Knowledge

You can apply what you have learned in this chapter by reading the following articles in *Applied H.R.M. Research* (www.radford.edu/~applyhrm).

Aamodt, M. G. (2004). Special issue on using MMPI-2 scale configurations in law enforcement selection: Introduction and meta-analysis. *Applied H.R.M. Research*, *9*(2), 41-52.

Godfrey, K. J., Bonds, A. S., Kraus, M. E., Wiener, M. R., & Toth, C. S. (1990). Freedom from stress: A meta-analytic view of treatment and intervention programs. *Applied H.R.M. Research, 1*(2), 67-80.

7. Factor Analysis

IMAGINE THE FOLLOWING SITUATIONS:

- A human resource manager asked her employees 50 questions about their attitudes toward work and is looking to find an easy way to summarize the responses to the 50 questions.
- An HR analyst has written a 100-item math test and is worried that the test may be tapping more than just math skills.
- A training specialist has evaluated her employees on 20 dimensions of communication skills but is worried that giving feedback on 20 dimensions will take too long and be too difficult to understand.
- An organization development specialist created a personality test to use in training workshops. He thinks his 200 questions tap five distinct personality dimensions.

In these situations, the four human resource professionals have one of two goals. Either they want to reduce a large amount of data (e.g., 50 attitude questions, 20 communication dimensions) into something more manageable, or they want to ensure that they are measuring the correct number of constructs (e.g., math skills, 5 personality dimensions). Factor analysis will help achieve both goals.

Factor analysis is a statistical technique that is extremely difficult to compute by hand, fairly easy to compute with a computer program such as SAS or SPSS, and fairly easy to understand when reading the results in a journal article. This chapter will focus on understanding the terminology and tables used in journal articles using factor analysis.

A factor analysis computes the similarity of responses to a series of questions and then determines groups of questions that seem to generate similar responses. For example, in a study on hobbies, interest in baseball, football, and basketball might fall into a "sports" group and interest in hiking, canoeing, and fishing might fall into an "outdoor" group.

These groupings are called *factors*. For each question, a *factor coefficient* is generated indicating the extent to which that question relates to each factor. These factor coefficients can be interpreted in much the same way as we would a correlation coefficient: the higher the coefficient, the greater the relationship between the question and the factor.

Determining the Number of Factors

If you have nine items in your factor analysis, you can potentially have nine factors if none of the items are related to each other. However, the goal of factor analysis is to reduce the number of items to a smaller number of meaningful factors. For a factor to be meaningful, it must explain a significant amount of the relationships among the items. This amount is called an *eigenvalue*; the higher the eigenvalue, the greater the amount of variance that is explained by that factor, and thus, the more important the factor. Most computer programs use, and most texts suggest, an eigenvalue of one as a default for keeping a factor. The decision regarding the ideal number of factors is guided by a need to balance simplicity (fewer factors) with precision (many factors accounting for the majority of the variance).

For example, suppose that we asked 100 students to use a five-point scale to rate how well they like nine different foods. As shown in Table 7.1, a factor analysis reveals that these nine foods represent three distinct factors, with eigenvalues for the factors of 1.96, 1.79, and 1.69. Note that these three eigenvalues are similar in magnitude, indicating that the three factors are of about equal importance. Contrast this similarity with the difference in eigenvalues shown in Tables 7.3 and 7.4.

Table 7.1
Factor Analysis of Favorite Foods

Food	Factor I	Factor II	Factor III
Carrots	- .08	**.64**	.12
Peas	- .01	**.84**	.02
Lima beans	.03	**.75**	- .03
Apples	- .21	.06	**.60**
Oranges	.11	- .18	**.87**
Plums	.08	.23	**.73**
Popcorn	**.80**	- .09	.05
Potato chips	**.83**	- .10	.00
Cracker jack	**.75**	.11	- .08
Eigenvalue	1.96	1.79	1.69

Table 7.2
Proposed Factor Loadings for a Personality Test

Item	Proposed Factors		
	Extraversion	Conscientiousness	Agreeableness
Outgoing	√		
Talkative	√		
Funny	√		
Sociable	√		
Reliable		√	
Dependable		√	
Timely		√	
Organized		√	
Loyal			√
Easy going			√
Accepting			√
Helpful			√

Table 7.3
Example of a Rotated and Unrotated Factor Matrix

Scale	No Rotation		Varimax Rotation		Quartimax Rotation	
	I	II	I	II	I	II
Verbal reasoning	.71	- .16	.72	.09	.73	.05
Math	.68	- .03	.65	.21	.66	.18
Grammar	.76	- .20	.79	.08	.79	.04
Vocabulary	.75	- .30	.81	- .01	.81	- .06
Perceptual speed	.46	.63	.23	.76	.27	.75
Manual speed	.27	.79	- .02	.83	.02	.83
Eigenvalues	2.27	1.33	2.27	1.33	2.27	1.33

For a factor analysis to be reliable, there needs to be data from a sufficient number of people. Almost every expert agrees that there should be data from at least 100 people. However, in determining a sufficient sample size, one also needs to consider the number of variables. Most experts agree that data from at least five people are needed for every variable. That is, if we are factor analyzing responses to 40 foods, we would need data from at least 200 people (40 items multiplied by 5 people). Some authors (e.g., Kachigan, 1986) suggest that there be ten people for every variable; or if there are more than 10 variables, the square of the number of variables is the minimum number of people needed. That is, if you have 15 variables, you need data from 225 people (15 times 15). These rules of thumb are the minimums: the more subjects you have, the better the reliability of your factor analysis.

There are times when a journal article will describe a study as a "confirmatory factor analysis." In such cases, rather than trying to explore the number of factors that exist, the researcher is trying to confirm that a set of items will yield a certain number of factors. The presumed number of factors is based either on previous research or on a theory. For example, suppose that a consultant created a 12-item personality test that he thought would yield scores on the three factors shown in Table 7.2. He would conduct his analysis to see if there were actually three factors and if the items loaded (had high factor coefficients) on the factors he thought they would.

Determining the Items Belonging to Each Factor

To determine the items that belong to each factor, we look at the size of the factor coefficients. Generally, for an item to belong to a factor, the factor coefficient must be .30 or higher. As you can see back in Table 7.1, popcorn (.80), potato chips (.83), and Cracker Jack (.75) belong to Factor 1; carrots (.64), peas (.84), and lima beans (.75) belong to Factor 2; and apples (.60), oranges (.87), and plums (.73) belong to Factor 3. Notice that some of the factor coefficients are negative. As you might remember from the chapter on correlation, a negative coefficient is not a bad thing: it simply tells us the direction of the relationship. For example, in Table 7.1, the negative loading of apples on Factor 1 (- .21) tells us that people who like apples are not as inclined to like the foods that load highly on Factor 1 (popcorn, potato chips, Cracker Jack).

Often, a negative loading is expected and helps define a factor. For example, we might add "shy" and "introverted" to the traits that form the extraversion factor in Table 7.2. Whereas, we would expect outgoing, talkative, funny, and sociable to have high positive factor coefficients; and we would expect shy and introverted to have high negative factor coefficients on the extraversion factor.

When describing the results of a factor analysis, researchers will often use the term *rotation*. Rotation is a statistical procedure that makes it easier to determine the items that belong to each factor. The most common rotations include varimax, equimax, oblimin, and quartimax; each of which has a different goal. For example, the goal of a varimax rotation is to have high factor coefficients for items that are relevant to the factor and very low coefficients for the other items. In contrast, the aim of a quartimax rotation is to increase the odds that an item will have a high factor coefficient on only one factor. It should be noted that a rotation only makes the factor analysis easier to interpret. It does not change the actual relationships among the items.

Table 7.3 shows the factor analysis of six scales from an ability test. Notice that without a rotation, perceptual speed and vocabulary have high loadings on both factors. After rotation, however, the factors are "cleaner," and each scale loads only on one factor, making the factors easier to interpret. Also notice that the factor loadings for the two types of rotations are almost identical, thus the type of rotation would not have mattered. This is not always the case.

Naming the Factors

Once we see the items that belong to a factor, we try to make sense of that factor by giving it a name. The example back in Table 7.1 should be easy —the three factors represent the food groups of vegetables, fruits, and junk food. Sometimes, however, naming the factors can be more challenging. A good example comes from the factor analysis of difficult employee types that was conducted by Raynes (1997). Raynes noticed that popular books on dealing with difficult people (e.g., Bramson, 1981; Brinkman & Kirshner, 1994) suggested that there are several types of difficult people such as tanks, snipers, whiners, yes people, no people, maybe people, gossipers, and know-it-alls. Raynes, who questioned whether there were actually so many types, factor analyzed supervisor ratings of employees' difficult behaviors and found that these behaviors could be reduced to the two factors shown in Table 7.4. What would you call these two factors? Raynes (1997) labeled Factor I aggressive behaviors and Factor II passive behaviors.

The Raynes study is a good example of the usefulness of

factor analysis. By reducing the number of variables from 10 to 2, Raynes was able to conduct a more efficient study of the validity of a test battery in screening applicants who might become problem employees. But more importantly, the factor analysis demonstrated that the popular belief that there are 10 separate types of difficult employees is not true. Instead, there is one type (aggressive) who gossips, disagrees, whines, throws tantrums, and uses sarcasm, and a second type (passive) who can't say no and won't speak up. Thus, rather than learning how to deal with 10 types of difficult people, we only need to learn how to handle two types.

Determining if the Factor Analysis is Any Good

With most statistics, we get a significance level that helps us determine the confidence we can place in our findings. With factor analysis, determining if the results are "significant" is a bit more difficult. One way to evaluate an exploratory factor analysis is to consider the amount of variance that is explained by the factors. This is done by summing the eigenvalues and then dividing by the number of items that were factor analyzed. For example, for the factor analysis shown in Table 7.1, after summing the eigenvalues (1.96 + 1.79 + 1.69) and dividing by the number of items (9), we see that 60.4% of the variance (5.44 ÷ 9) was accounted for by the three factors. The two factors in Table 7.3 account for 55.9% of the variance. At a minimum, we want this percentage to be above 50.

If a factor analysis is done to confirm that a certain number of factors exist, there are a host of statistics to test how well the obtained factor analysis results "fit" the expected results. These "goodness-of-fit" indexes range in value from 0-1: the closer to one, the better the fit. An index of .90 is considered the acceptable level (Bryant & Yarnold, 1995).

Table 7.4

Factor Analysis of Difficult People

Difficult Behavior	Factor I	Factor II
Gossiping	.85	.07
Disagreeing with everyone	.84	.00
Yelling	.74	- .10
Acting like a know-it-all	.73	.00
Whining	.73	- .02
Saying no to everything	.66	.38
Using sarcasm	.50	.09
Not making up their mind	.43	.69
Not speaking up	.04	.78
Agreeing to everything	- .21	.63
Eigenvalues	3.97	1.62

Applying Your Knowledge

You can apply what you have learned in this chapter by reading the following articles in *Applied H.R.M. Research* (www.radford.edu/~applyhrm).

Conte, J. M., Ringenbach, K. L., Moran, S. K., & Landy, F. J. (2001). Criterion-validity evidence for time urgency: Associations with burnout, organizational commitment, and job involvement in travel agents. *Applied H.R.M. Research, 6*(2), 129-134.

Franz, T. M. & Norton, S. D. (2001). Investigating business casual dress policies: Questionnaire development and exploratory research. *Applied H.R.M. Research, 6*(2), 79-94.

Raynes, B. L. (2001). Predicting difficult employees: The relationship between vocational interests, self-esteem, and problem communication styles. *Applied H.R.M. Research, 6*(1), 33-66.

References

Aamodt, M. G. (2007). *Applied Industrial/Organizational Psychology (5thed.).* Belmont, CA: Wadsworth.

Aamodt, M. G., & Williams, F. (2005, April). *Reliability, validity, and adverse impact of references and letters of recommendation.* Paper presented at the 20th annual meeting of the Society for Industrial and Organizational Psychology, Los Angeles, CA.

Allard, G., Butler, J., Faust, D., & Shea, T. M. (1995). Errors in had scoring objective personality tests: The case of the Personality Diagnostic Questionnaire. *Professional Psychology: Research and Practice, 26*(3), 304-308.

Alliger, G. M., Tannenbaum, S. I., Bennett, W., Traver, H., & Shotland, A. (1997). A meta-analysis of the relations among training criteria. *Personnel Psychology, 50*(2), 341-358.

Arthur, W., Bennett, W., & Huffcutt, A. I. (2001). *Conducting meta-analysis using SAS.* Mahwah, NJ: Erlbaum.

Baltes, B. B., Briggs, T. E., Huff, J. W., Wright, J. A., and Neuman, G. A. (1999). Flexible and compressed work-week schedules: A meta-analysis of their effects on work-related criteria. *Journal of Applied Psychology, 84*(4), 496-513.

Beall, G. E. (1991). Validity of weighted application blanks across four job criteria. *Applied H.R.M. Research, 2*(1), 18-26.

Bramson, R. (1981). *Dealing with difficult people.* New York: Dell Publishing.

Brinkman, R., & Kirschner, R. (1994). *Dealing with people you can't stand.* New York: McGraw-Hill.

Bryant, F. B., & Yarnold, P. R. (1995). Principal-components analysis and exploratory and confirmatory factor analysis. In Grimm, L. G., & Yarnold, P. R. (Eds.) *Reading and understanding multivariate statistics.* Washington, D. C.: American Psychological Association.

Conway, J. M., & Huffcutt, A. I. (1997). Psychometric properties of multi-source performance ratings: A meta-analysis of subordinate, supervisor, peer, and self-ratings. *Human Performance, 10*(4), 331-360.

Cooper-Hakim, A., & Viswesvaran, C. (2005). The construct of work commitment: Testing an integrative framework. *Psychological Bulletin, 131*(2), 241-259.

References

Gaugler, B.B., Rosenthal, D. B., Thornton, G. C., & Bentson, C. (1987). Meta-analysis of assessment center validity. *Journal of Applied Psychology, 72,* 493-511.

Griffeth, R. W., Hom, P. W., & Gaertner, S. (2000). A meta-analysis of antecedents and correlates of employee turnover: Update, moderator tests, and research implications for the next millennium. *Journal of Management, 26*(3), 463-488.

Huffcutt, A. I., & Arthur, W. (1994). Hunter and Hunter (1984) revisited: Interview validity for entry-level jobs. *Journal of Applied Psychology, 79*(2), 184-190.

Hunter, J. E., & Schmidt, F. L. (1990). *Methods of meta-analysis: Correcting error and bias in research findings.* Newbury Park, CA: Sage Publications.

Judge, T. A., Thoresen, C. J., Bono, J. E., & Patton, G. K. (2001). The job satisfaction-job performance relationship: A qualitative and quantitative review. *Psychological Bulletin, 127*(3), 376-407.

Kachigan, S. K. (1986). *Statistical analysis.* NY: Radius Press.

Koslowsky, M., Sagie, A., Krausz, M., & Singer, A. H. (1997). Correlates of employee lateness: Some theoretical considerations. *Journal of Applied Psychology, 82*(1), 79-88.

Mathieu, J. E., & Zajac, D. M. (1990). A review and meta-analysis of the antecedents, correlates, and consequences of organizational commitment. *Psychological Bulletin, 108*(1), 171-194.

McDaniel, M. A., Morgeson, F. P., Finnegan, E. B., Campion, M. A., & Braverman, E. P. (2001). Use of situational judgment tests to predict performance: A clarification of the literature. *Journal of Applied Psychology, 86*(4), 730-740.

Ones, D.S., Viswesveran, C., & Schmidt, F. L. (1993). Comprehensive meta-analysis of integrity test validities: Findings for personnel selection and theories of job performance. *Journal of Applied Psychology, 78*(4), 679-703

Quinones, M.A., Ford, J. K., & Teachout, M. S. (1995). The relationship between work experience and job performance: A conceptual and meta-analytic review. *Personnel Psychology, 48*(4), 887-910.

Raynes, B. L. (1997). Screening for difficult people. *Assessment Council News,* October, 8-11.

Rosenthal, R. (1984). *Meta-analytic procedures for social research.* Beverly Hills, CA: Sage Publications.

Roth, P. L., Bevier, C. A., Switzer, F. S., & Schippmann, J. S. (1996). Meta-analyzing the relationship between grades and job performance. *Journal of Applied Psychology, 81*(5), 548-556.

Roth, P. L., Bobko, P., & McFarland, L. A. (2005). A meta-analysis of work sample test validity: Updating and integrating some classic literature. *Personnel Psychology, 58*(4), 1009-1037

Schmidt, F. L., & Hunter, J. E. (1998). The validity and utility of selection methods in personnel psychology: Practical and theoretical implications of 85 years of research findings. *Psychological Bulletin, 124*(2), 262-274.

Tett, R. P., Jackson, D. N., Rothstein, M., & Reddon, J. R. (1994). Meta-analysis of personality-job performance relations: A reply to Ones, Mount, Barrick, & Hunter. *Personnel Psychology, 47*(1), 157-172.

Viswesvaran, C., Ones, D. S., & Schmidt, F. L. (1996). Comparative analysis of the reliability of job performance ratings. *Journal of Applied Psychology, 81*(5), 557-574.

Index